Shakespeare said,

"Let's kill all the lawyers!"

Henry VI, Part IV, ii, 86

But *then*
what do we do
with them?

Now...

What to do with a Dead Lawyer

■ At home ■ At work
■ At play ■ On the go

By Bill Berger and Ricardo Martinez

1❿ Ten Speed Press

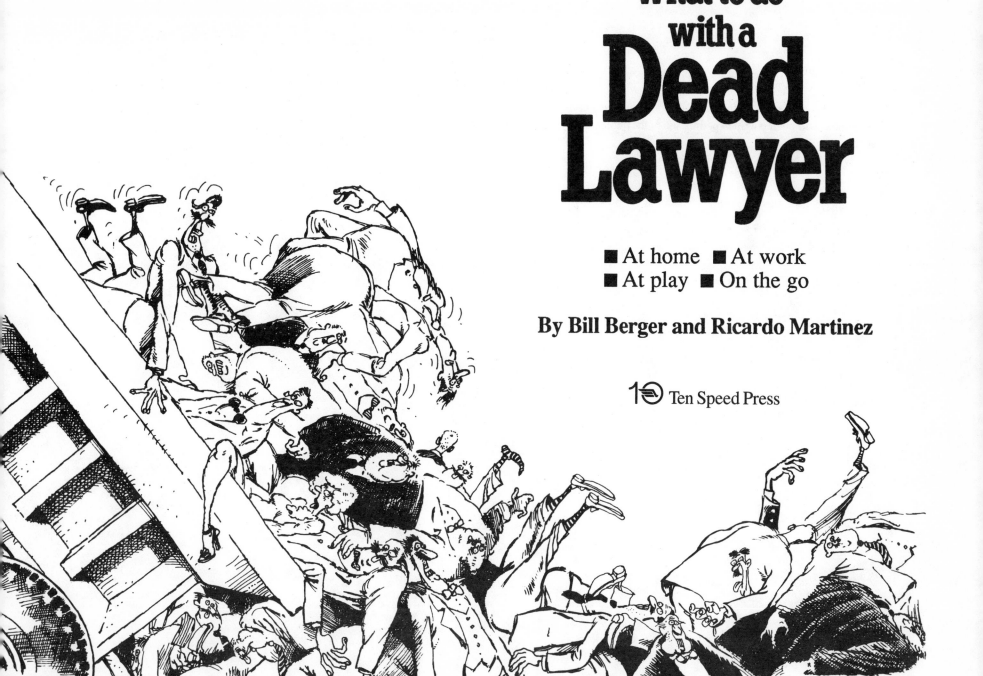

TEN SPEED PRESS
P O Box 7123
Berkeley, California 94707

Printed in the United States of America

1 2 3 4 5 — 92 91 90 89 88

Featuring —

Personal Injury Lawyers

Criminal Defense Lawyers

Environmental Lawyers

Labor Lawyers

Railroad Lawyers

Estate Planning Lawyers

Divorce Lawyers

Corporate Lawyers

Sports Lawyers

Auto Insurance Lawyers

Real Estate Lawyers

Medical Malpractice Lawyers

. . . And more!

At home

Adoption Lawyer

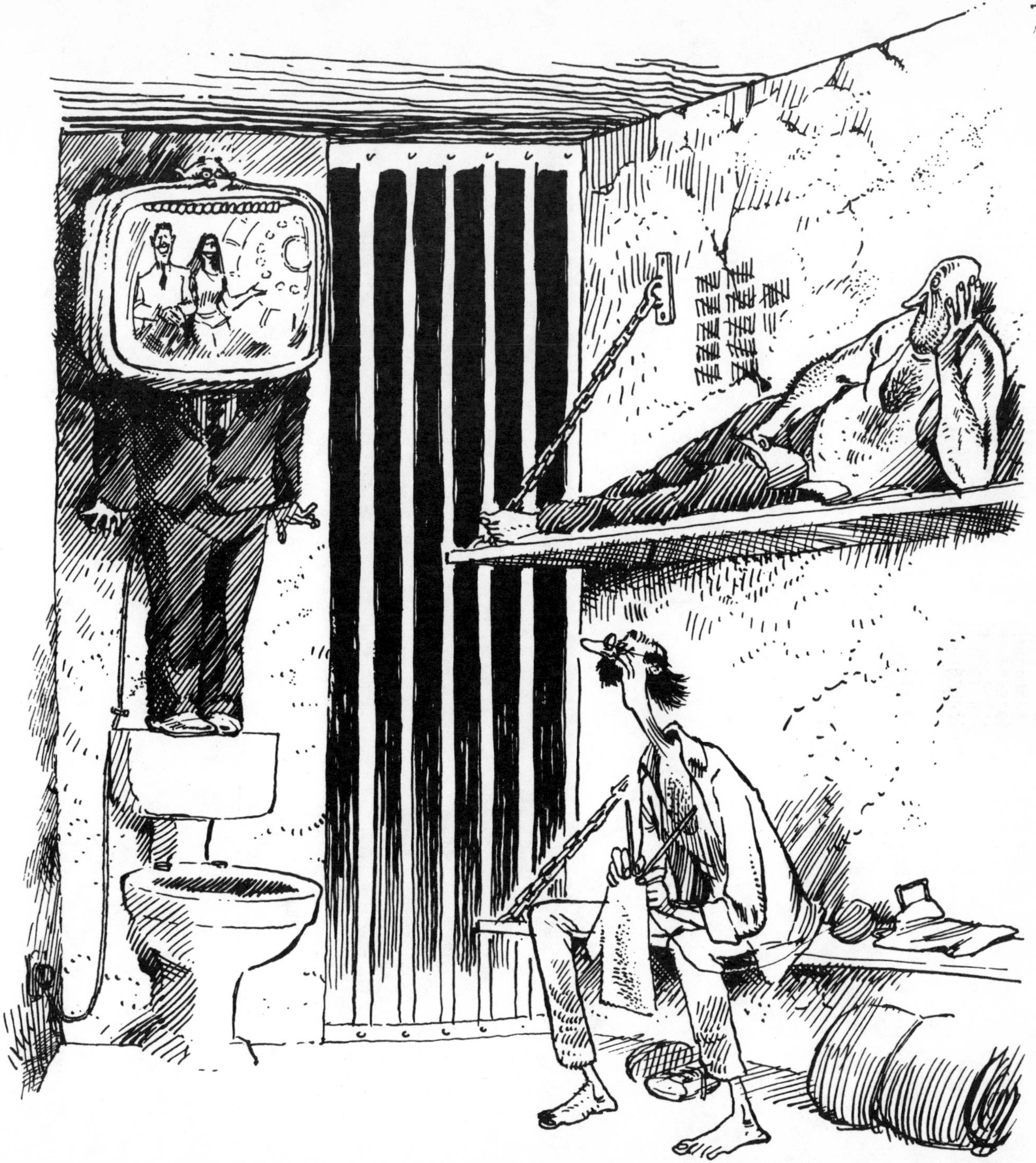

Civil Liberties Lawyer

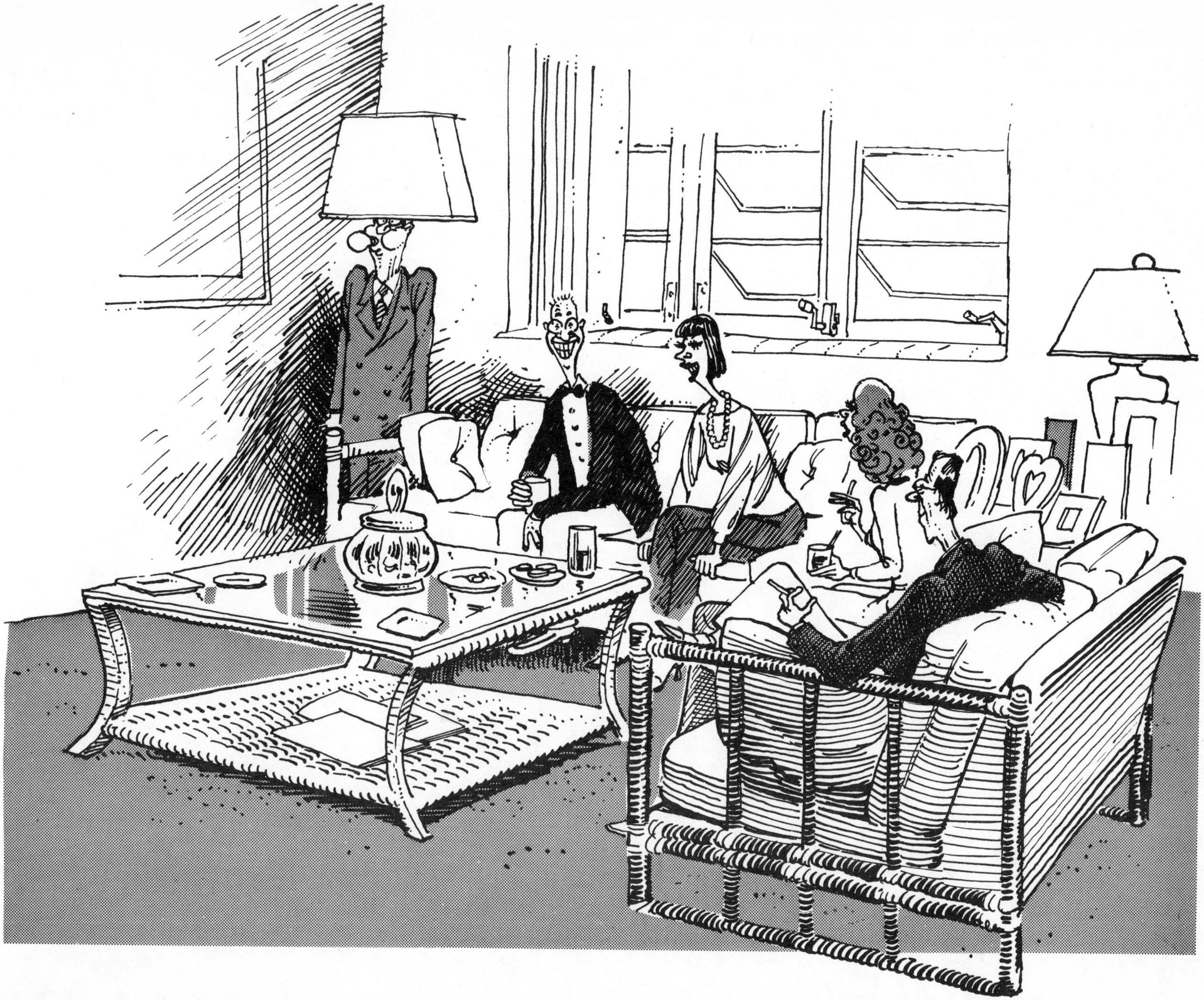

Electric Company's Lawyer

Ex-husband's Lawyer

Ex-wife's Lawyer

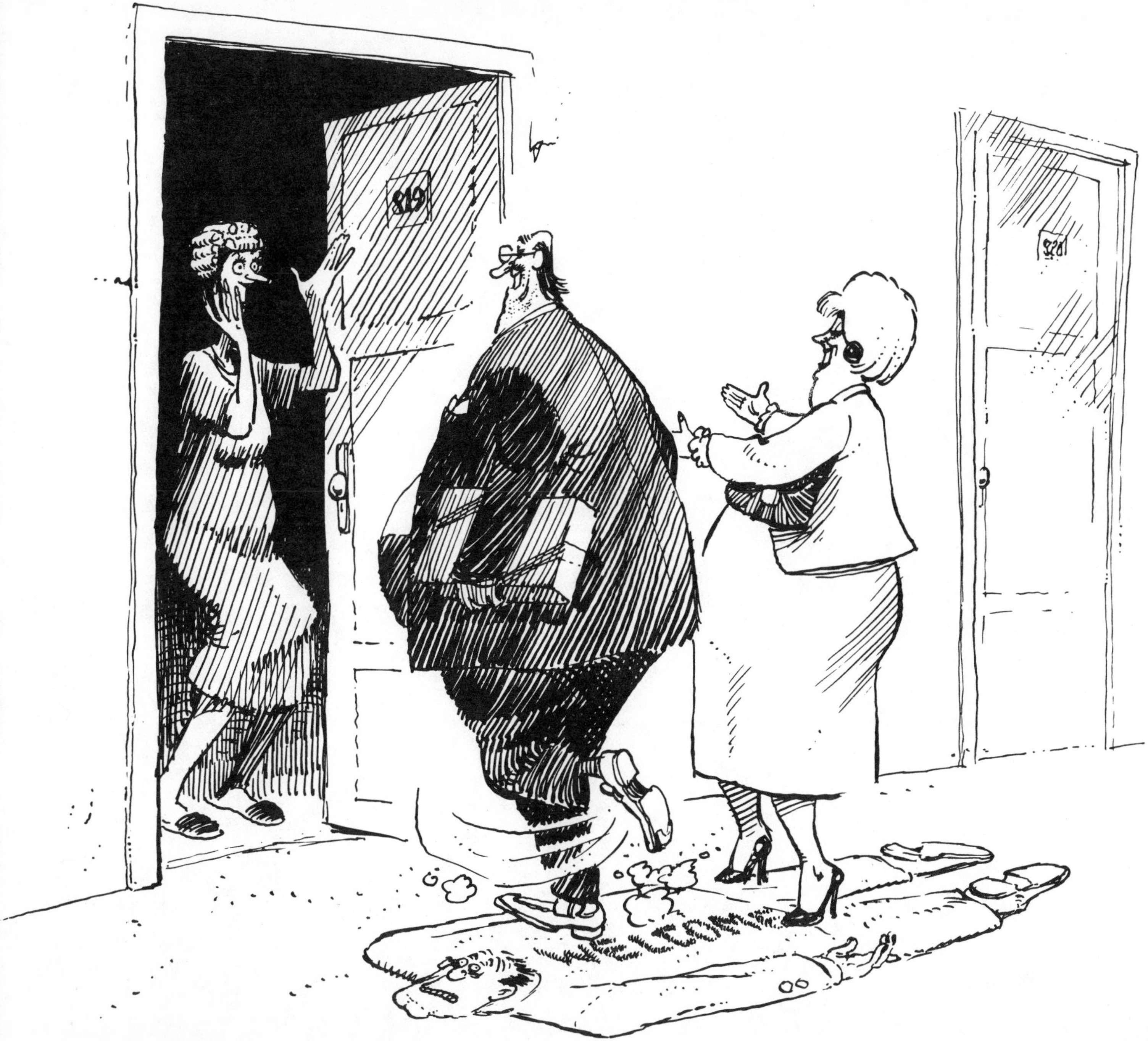

Landlord's Lawyer

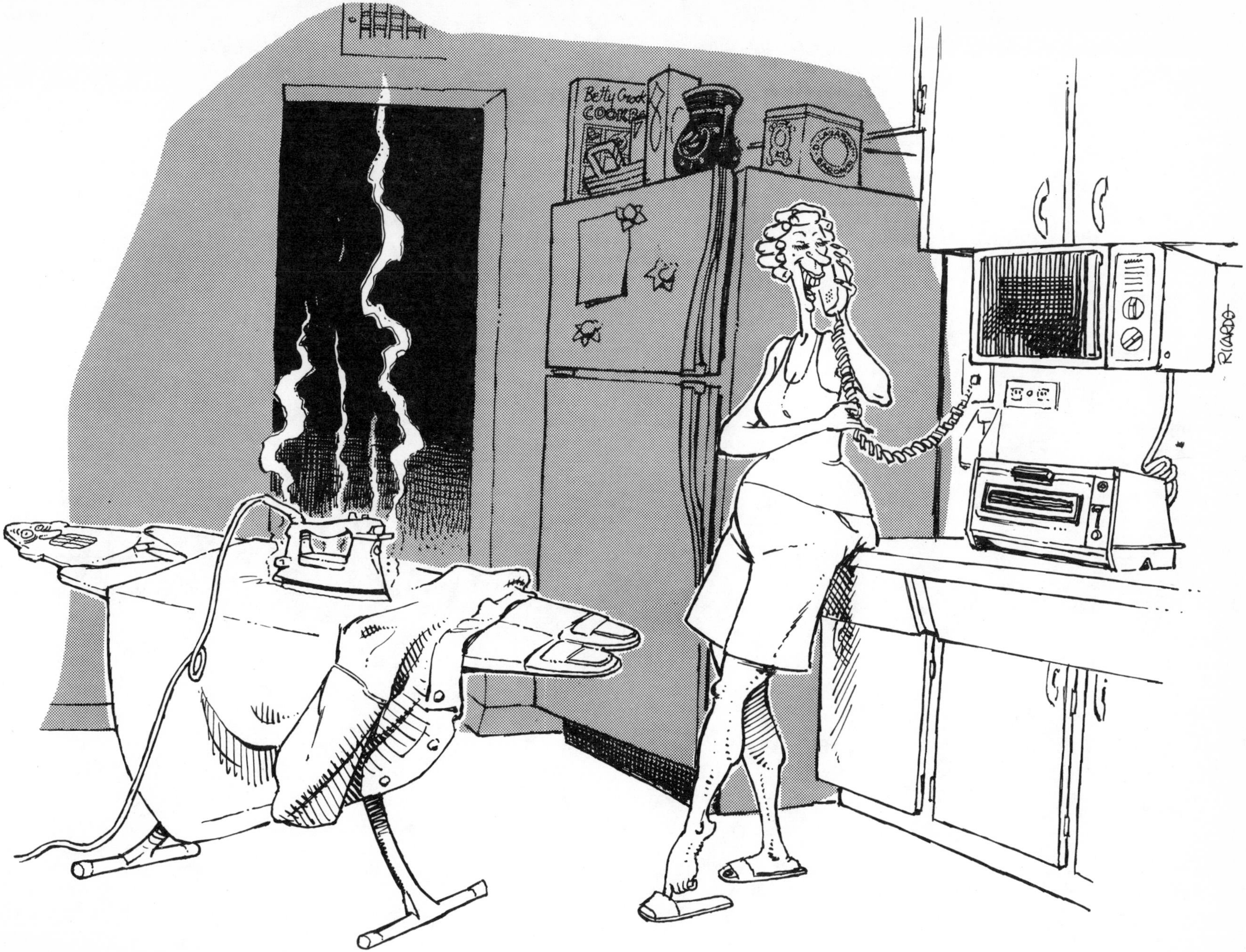
RICARDO

Products Liability Lawyer

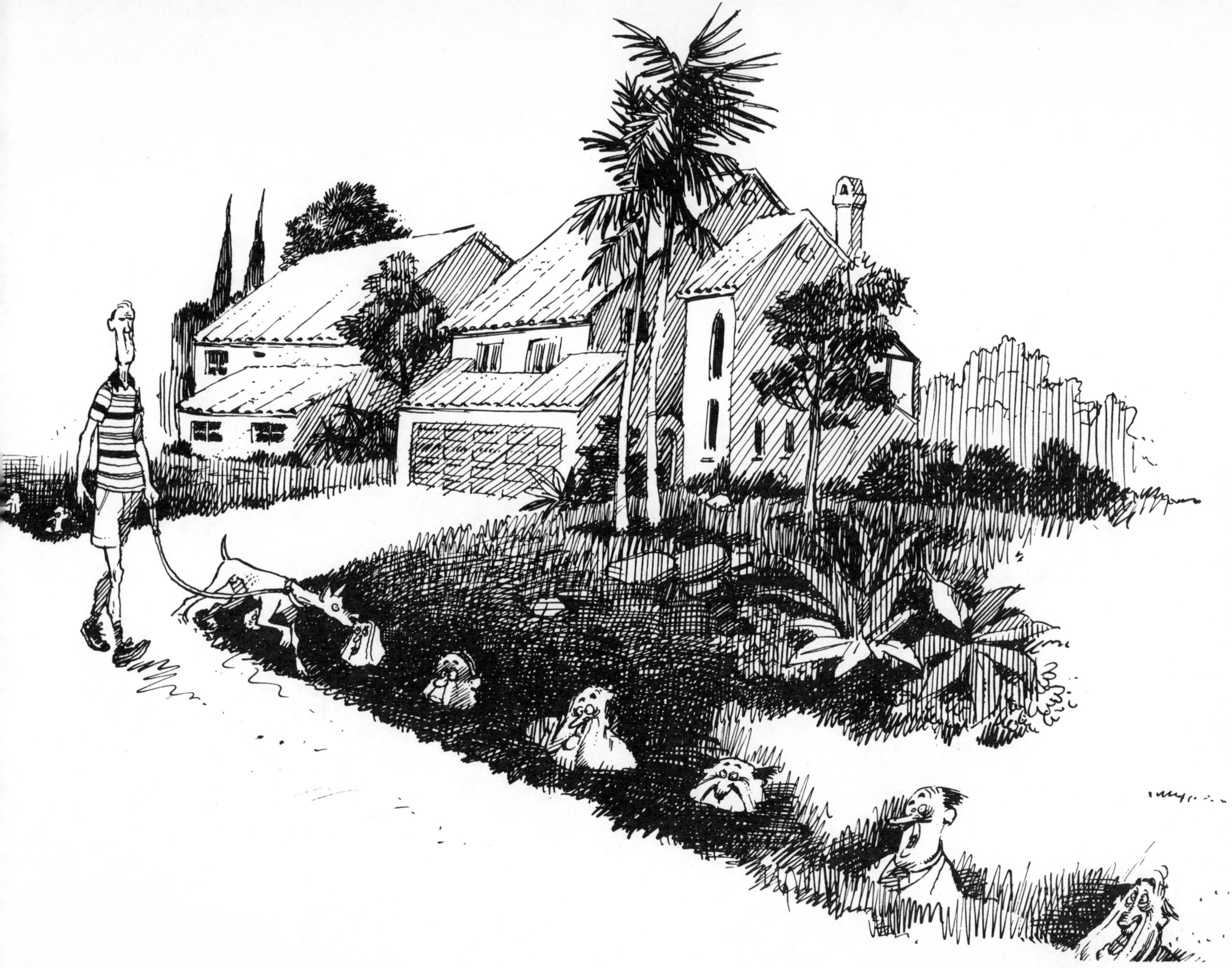

Real Estate Lawyers

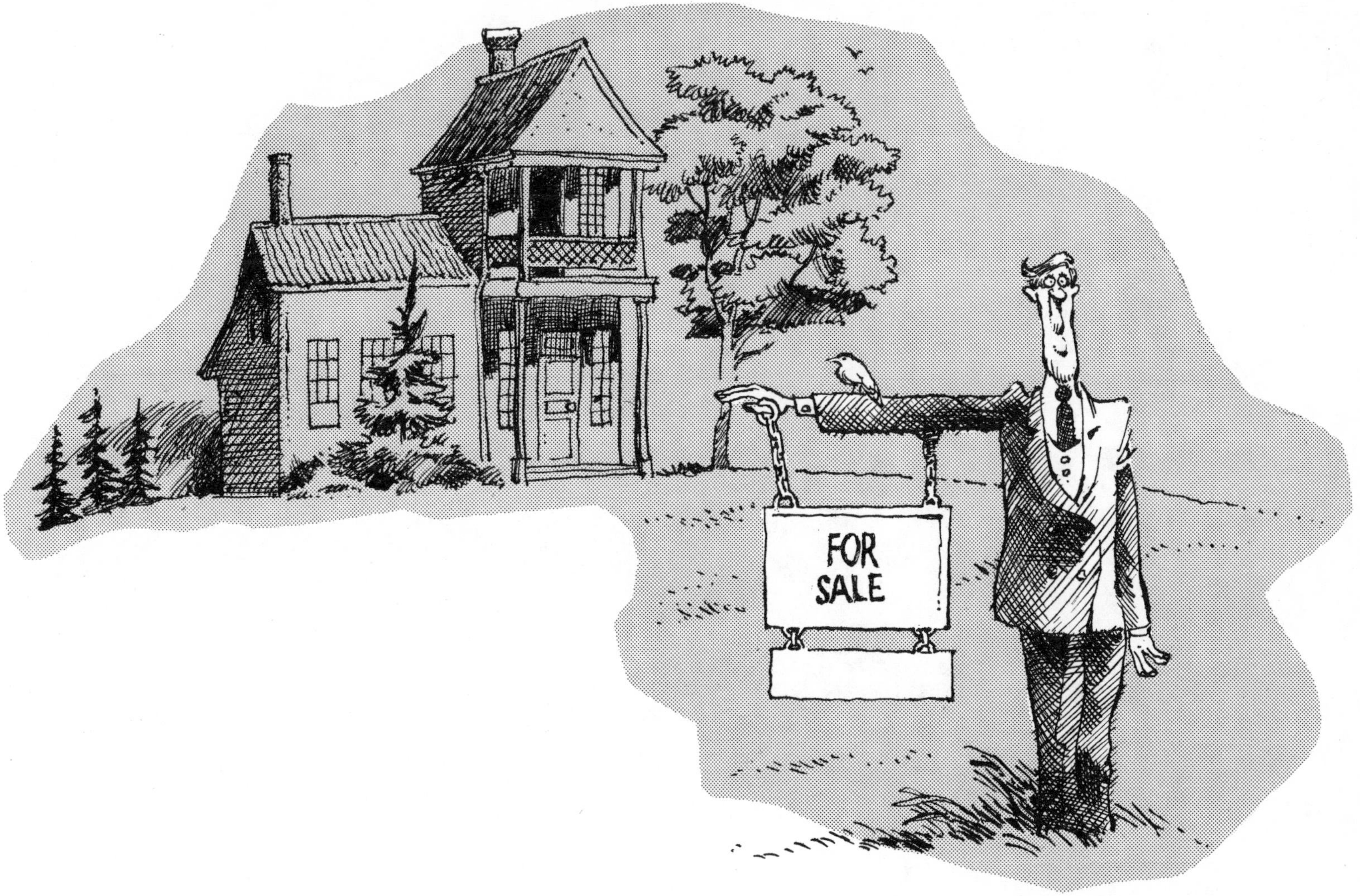
FOR
SALE

Realtor's Lawyer

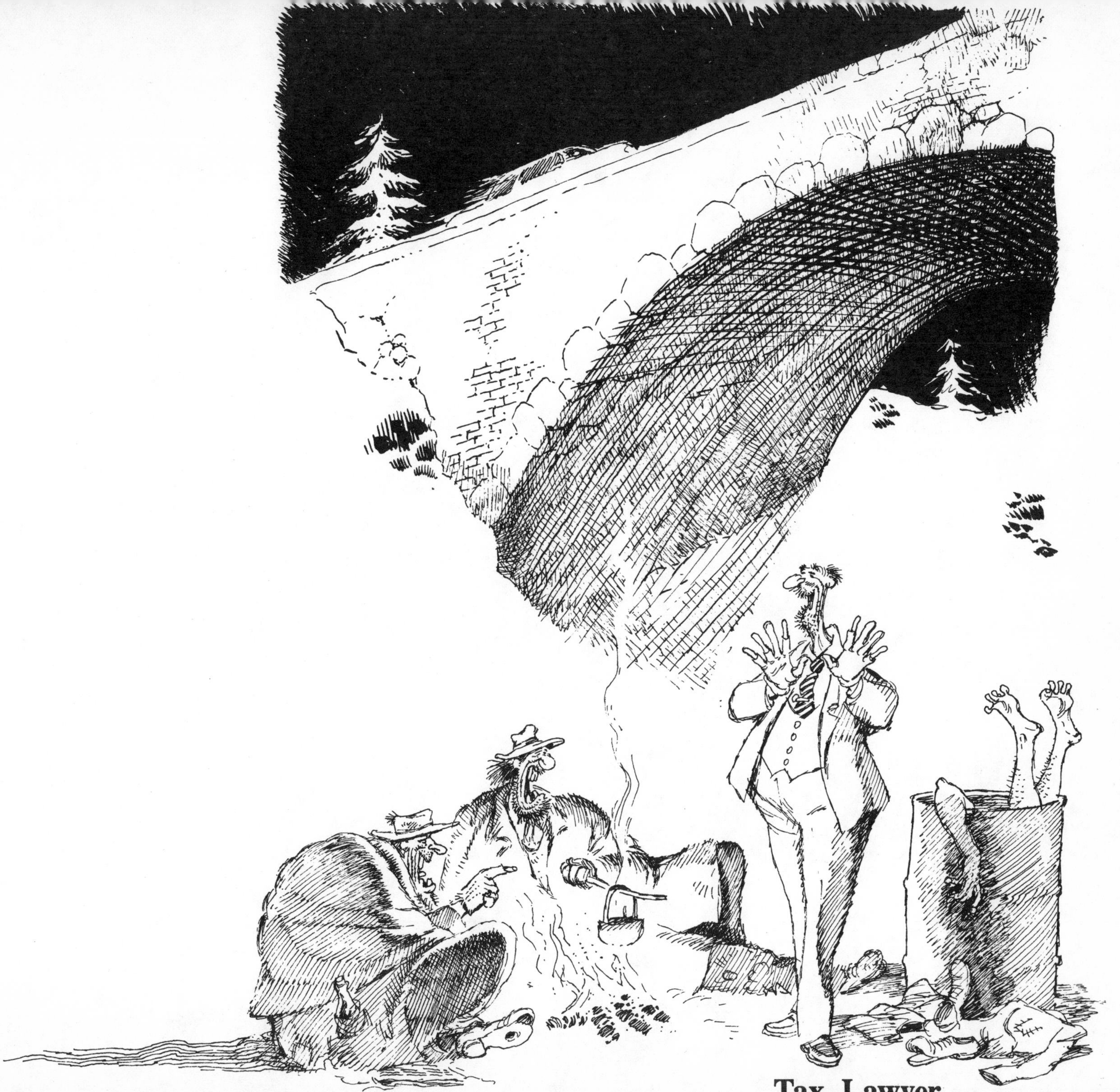

Tax Lawyer

Trial Lawyer

At work

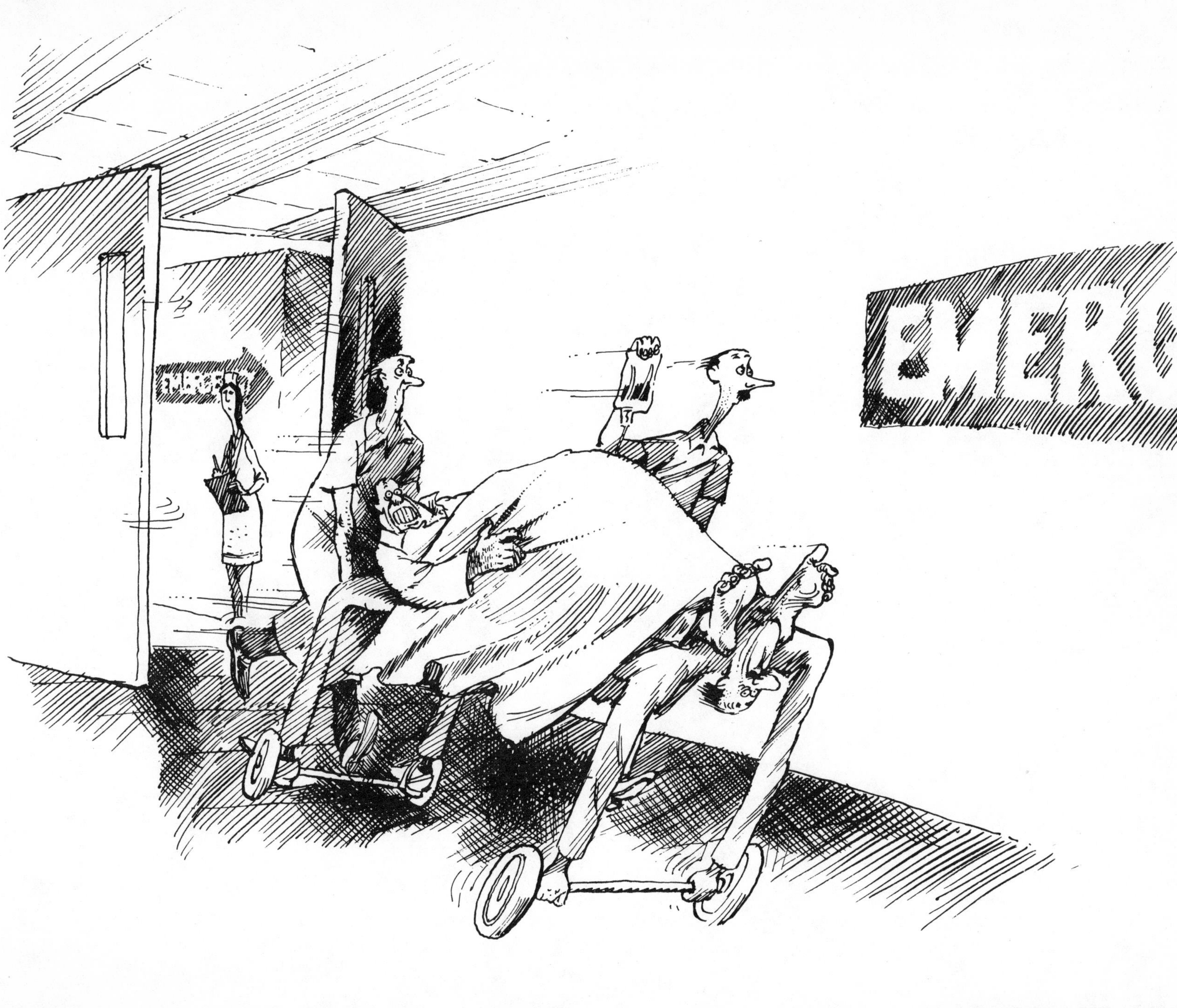
EMERG

Ambulance Chaser

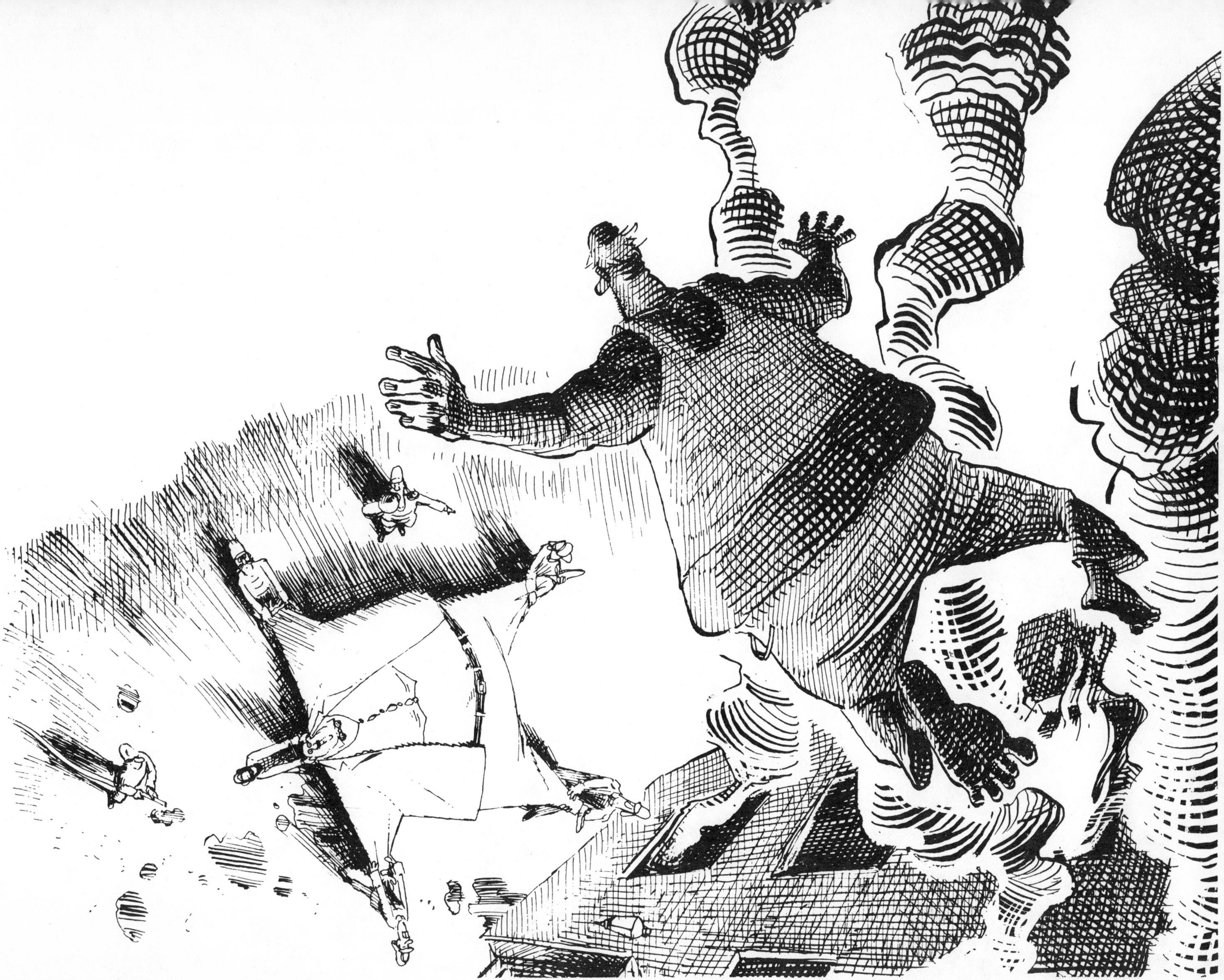

Architect's Lawyer

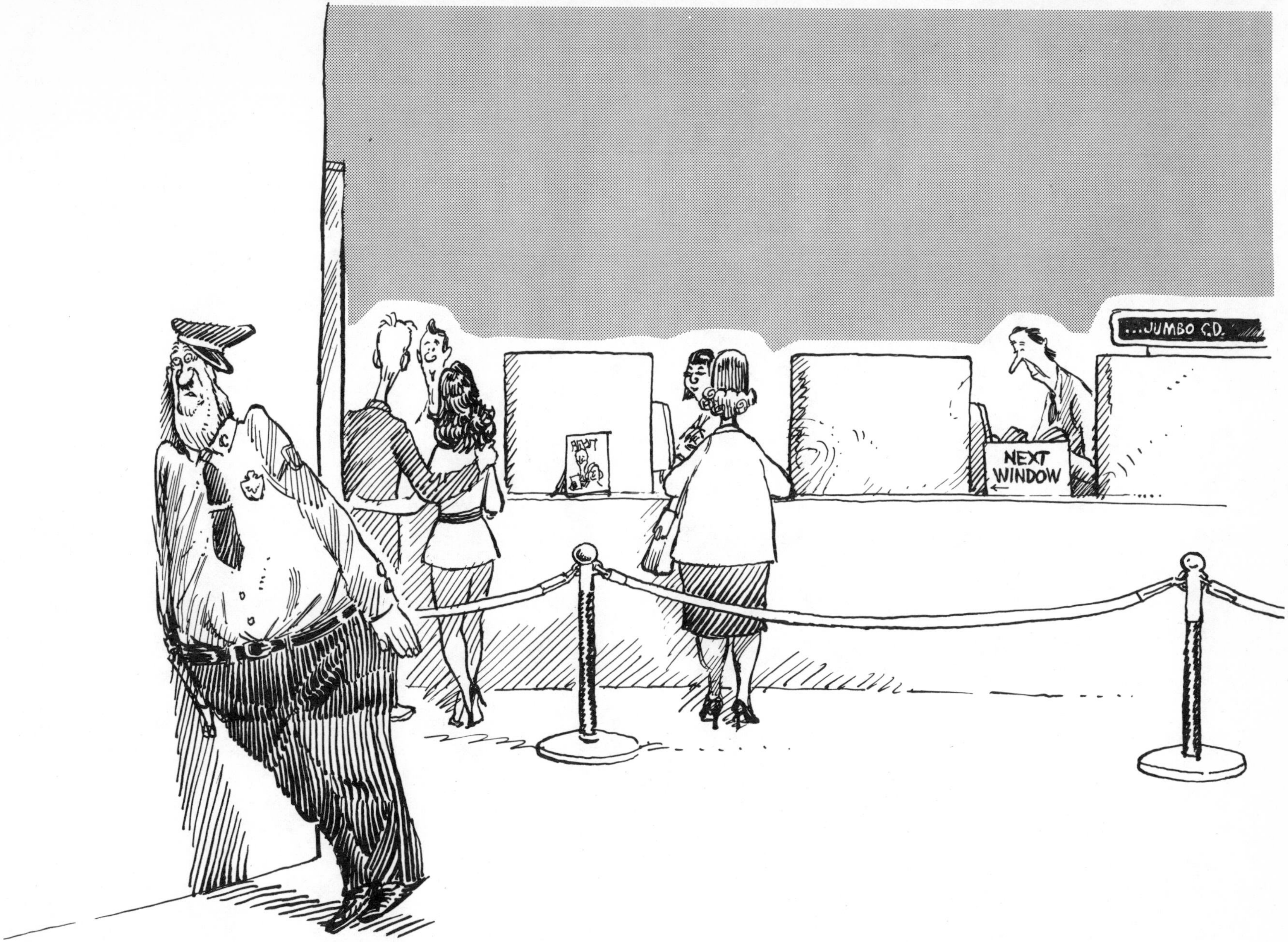

...JUMBO C.D.
NEXT WINDOW

Bank's Lawyer

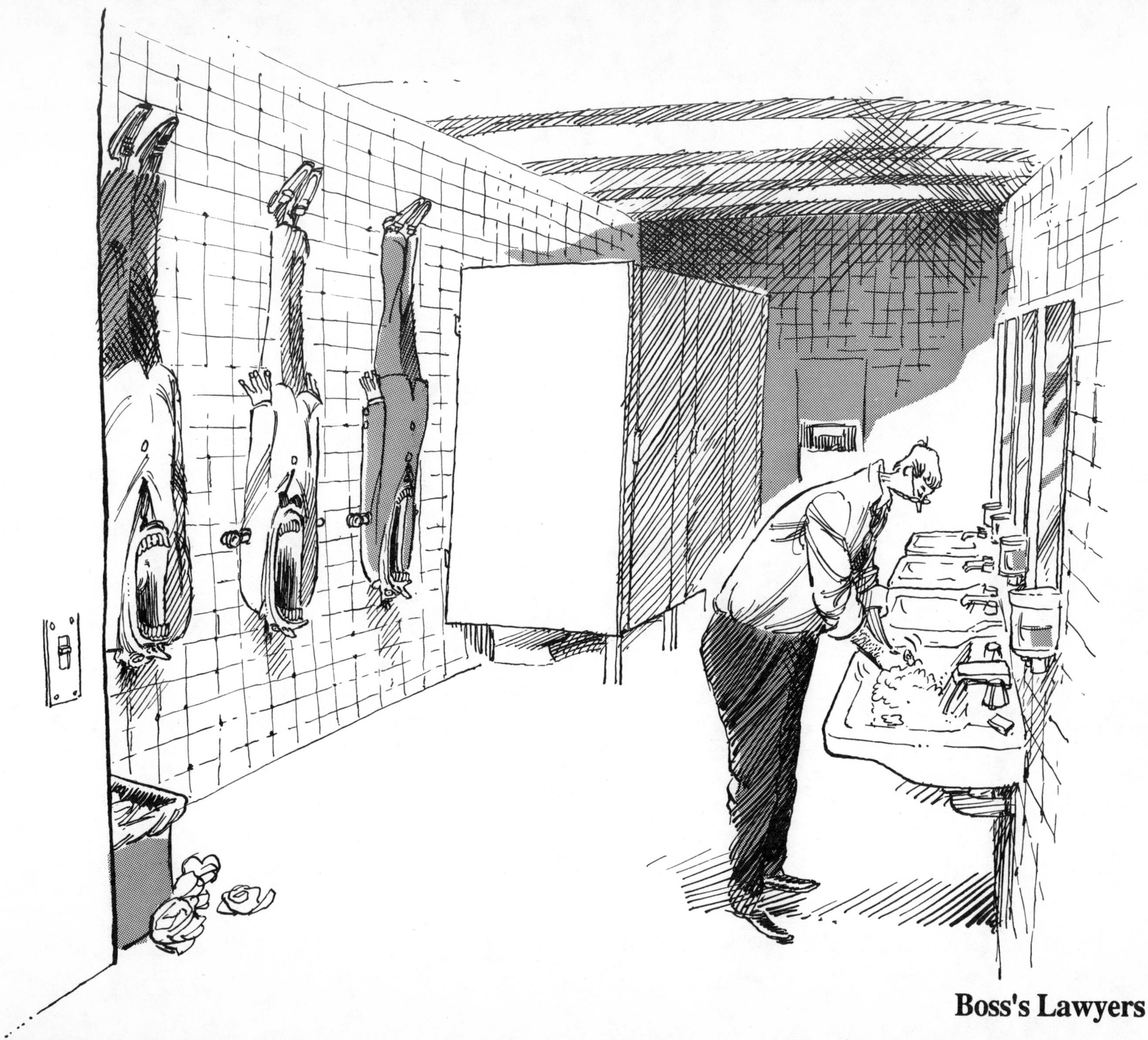

Boss's Lawyers

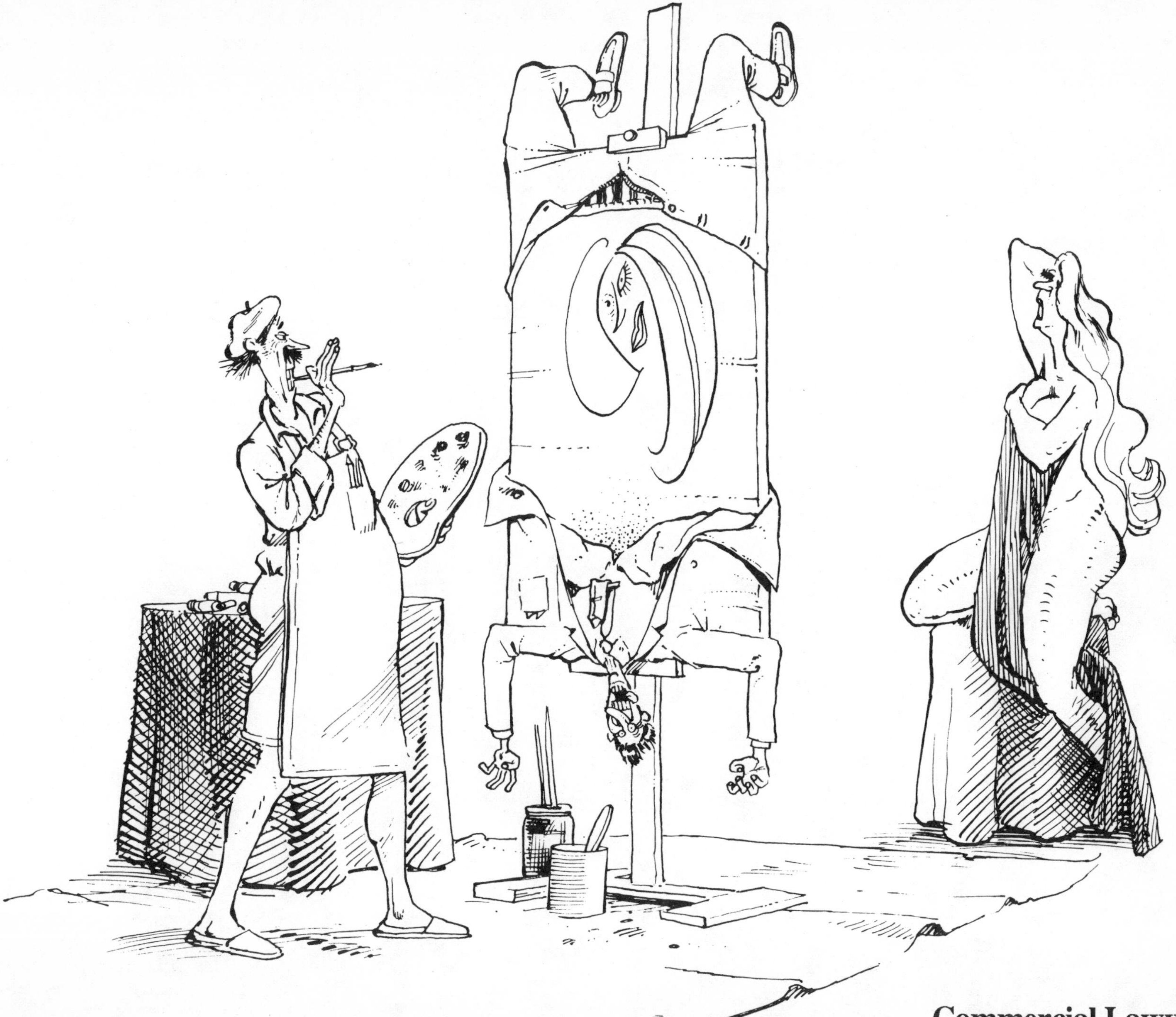

Commercial Lawyer

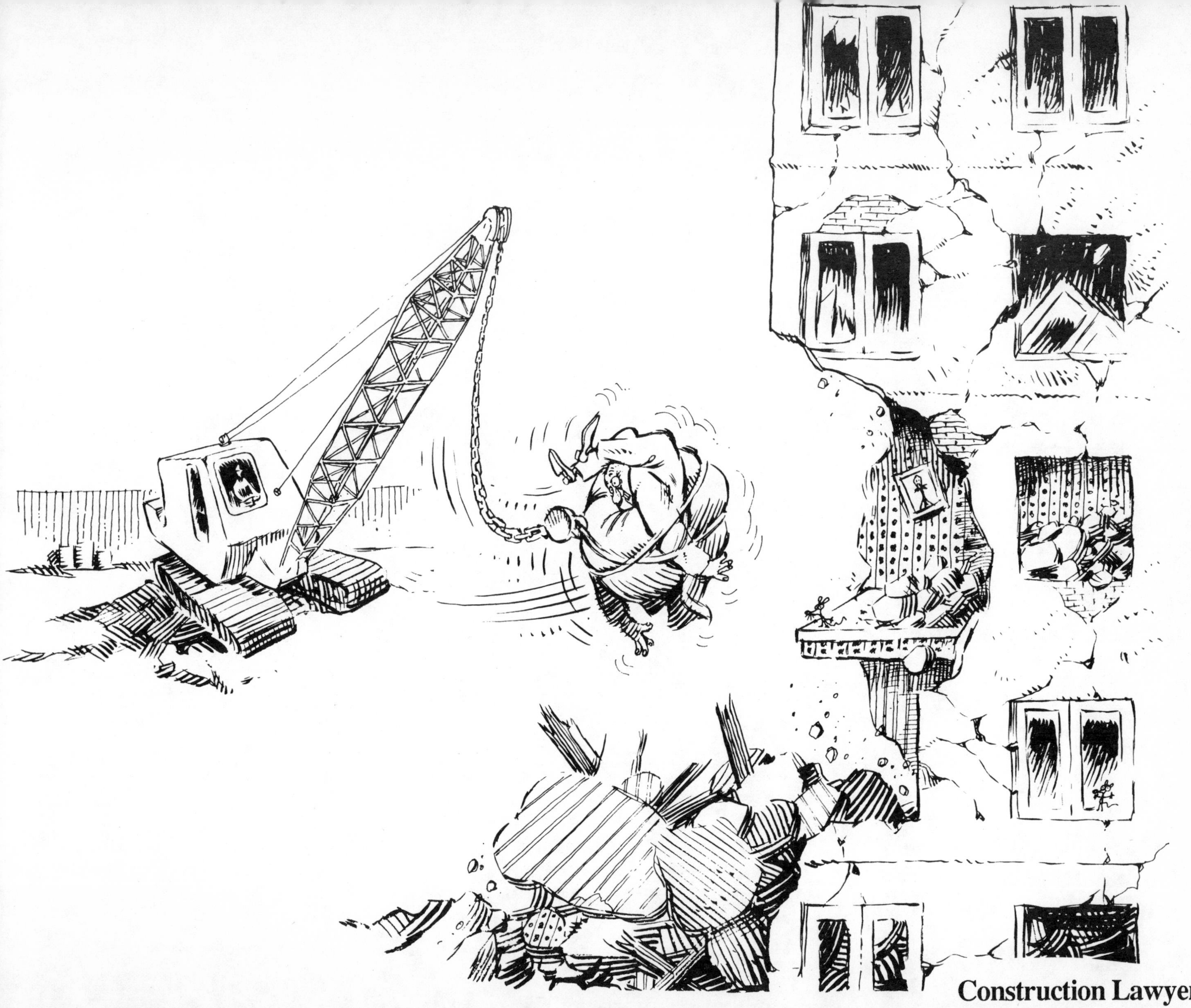

Construction Lawyer

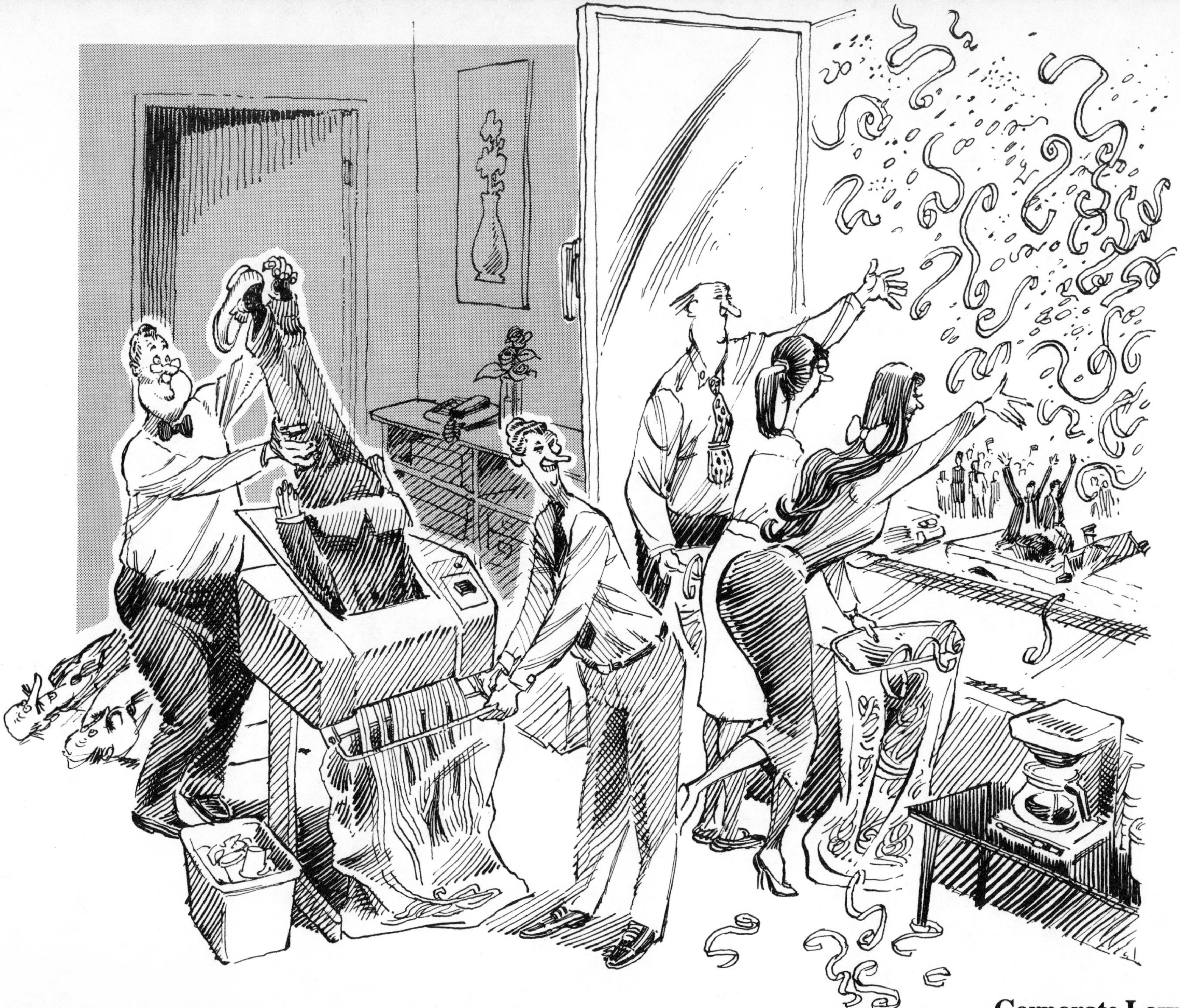

Corporate Lawyers

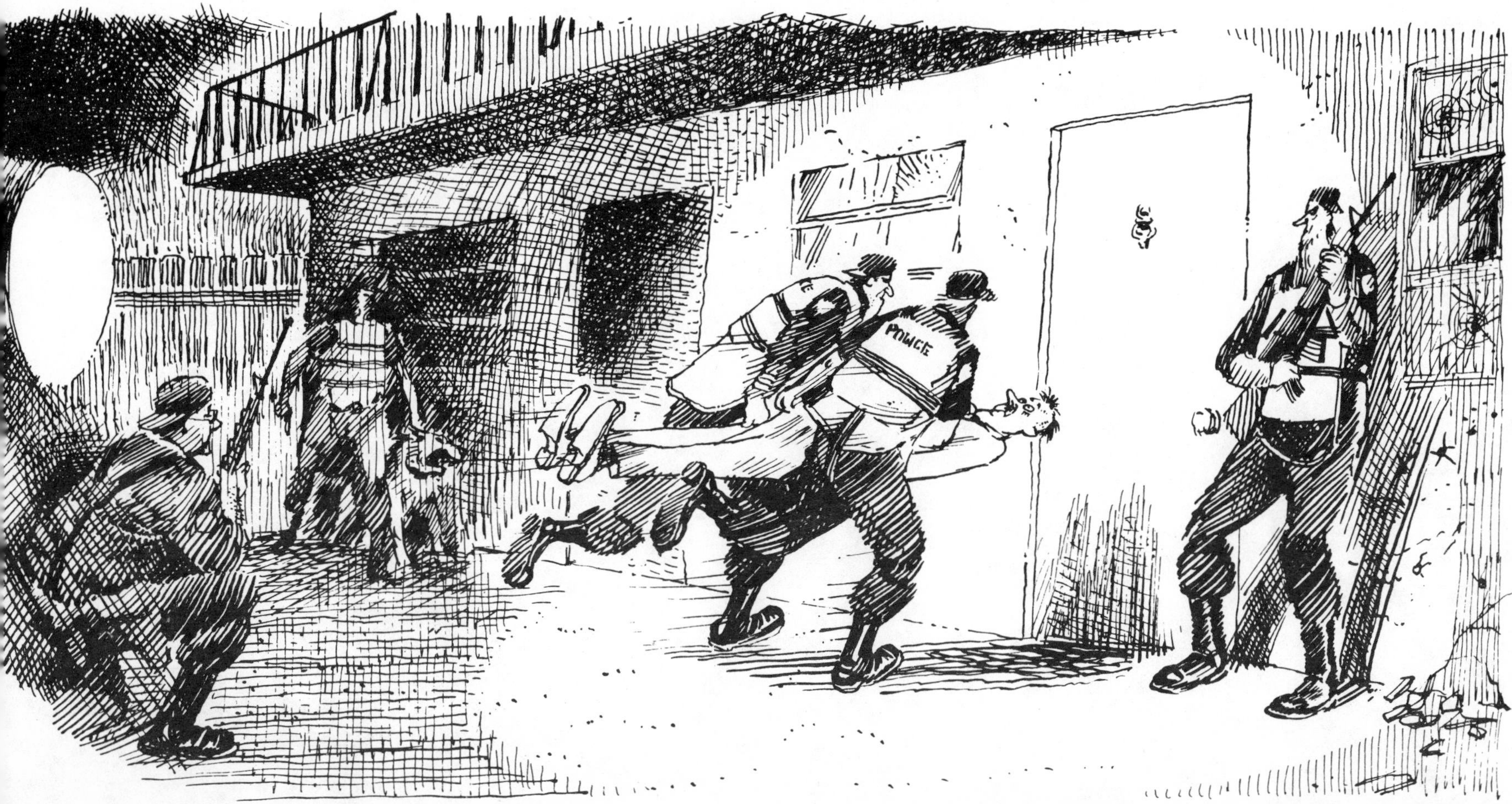
POLICE

Criminal Defense Lawyer

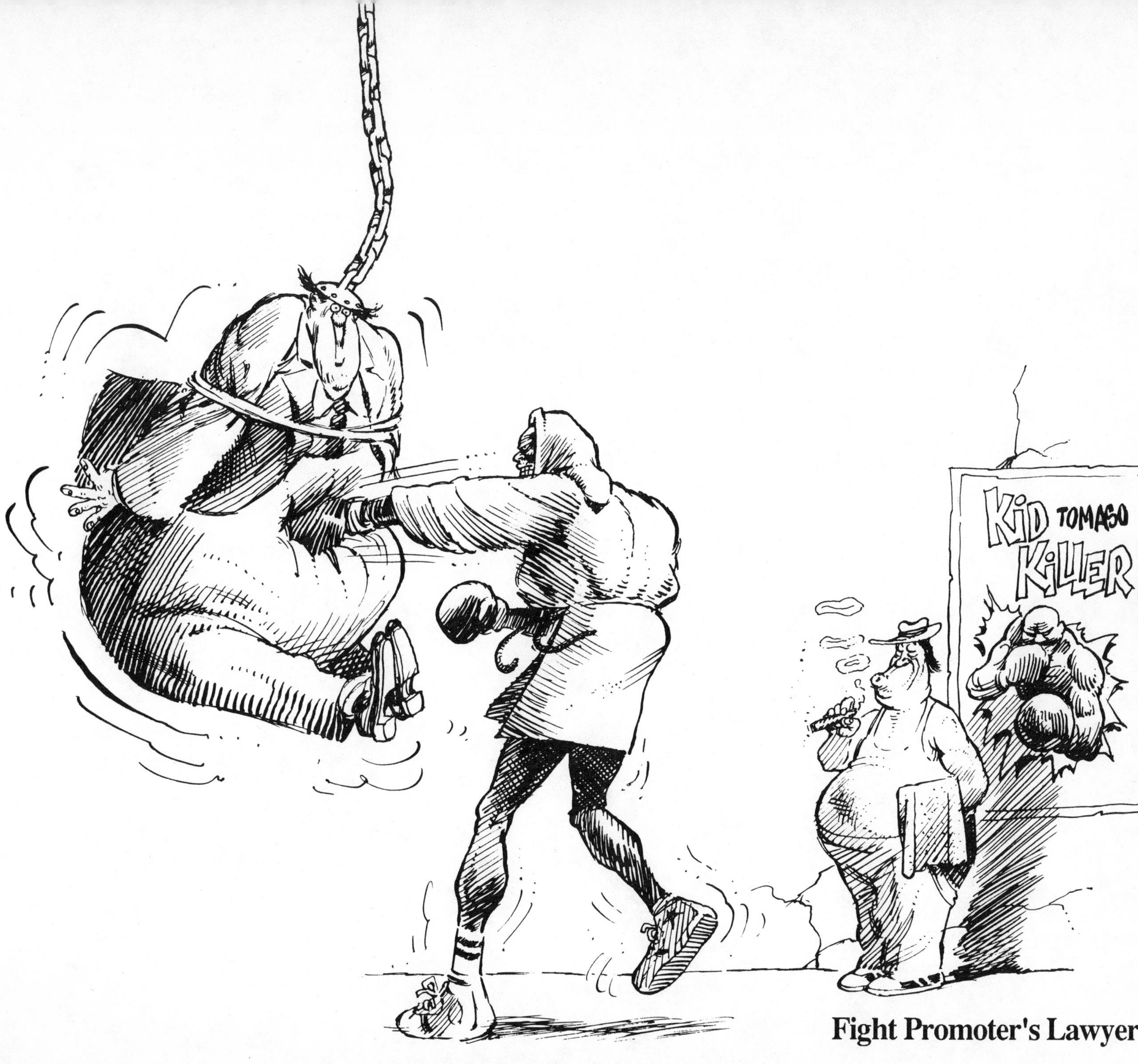
KID TOMASO
KILLER

Fight Promoter's Lawyer

Literary Lawyers

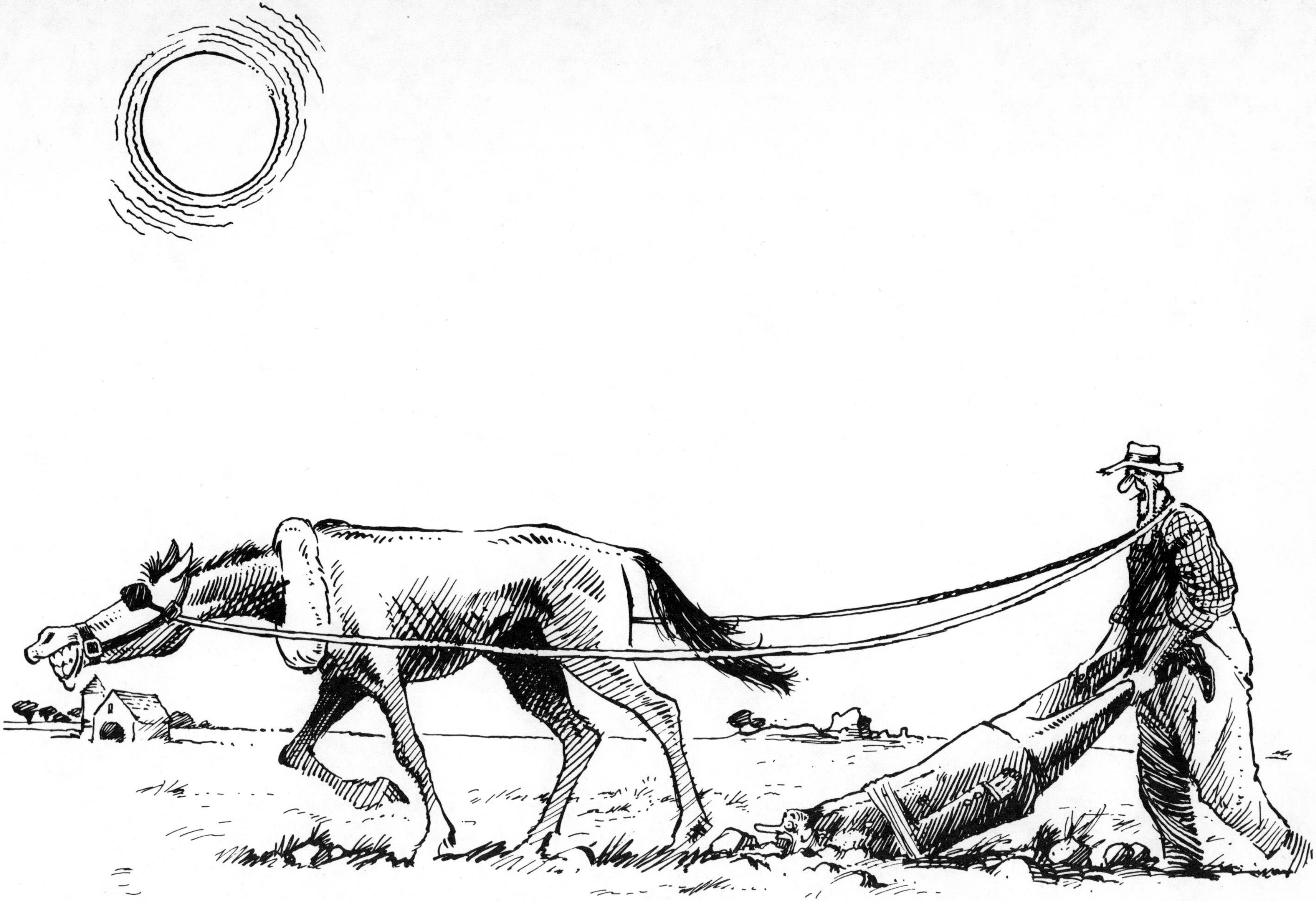

Government Lawyer

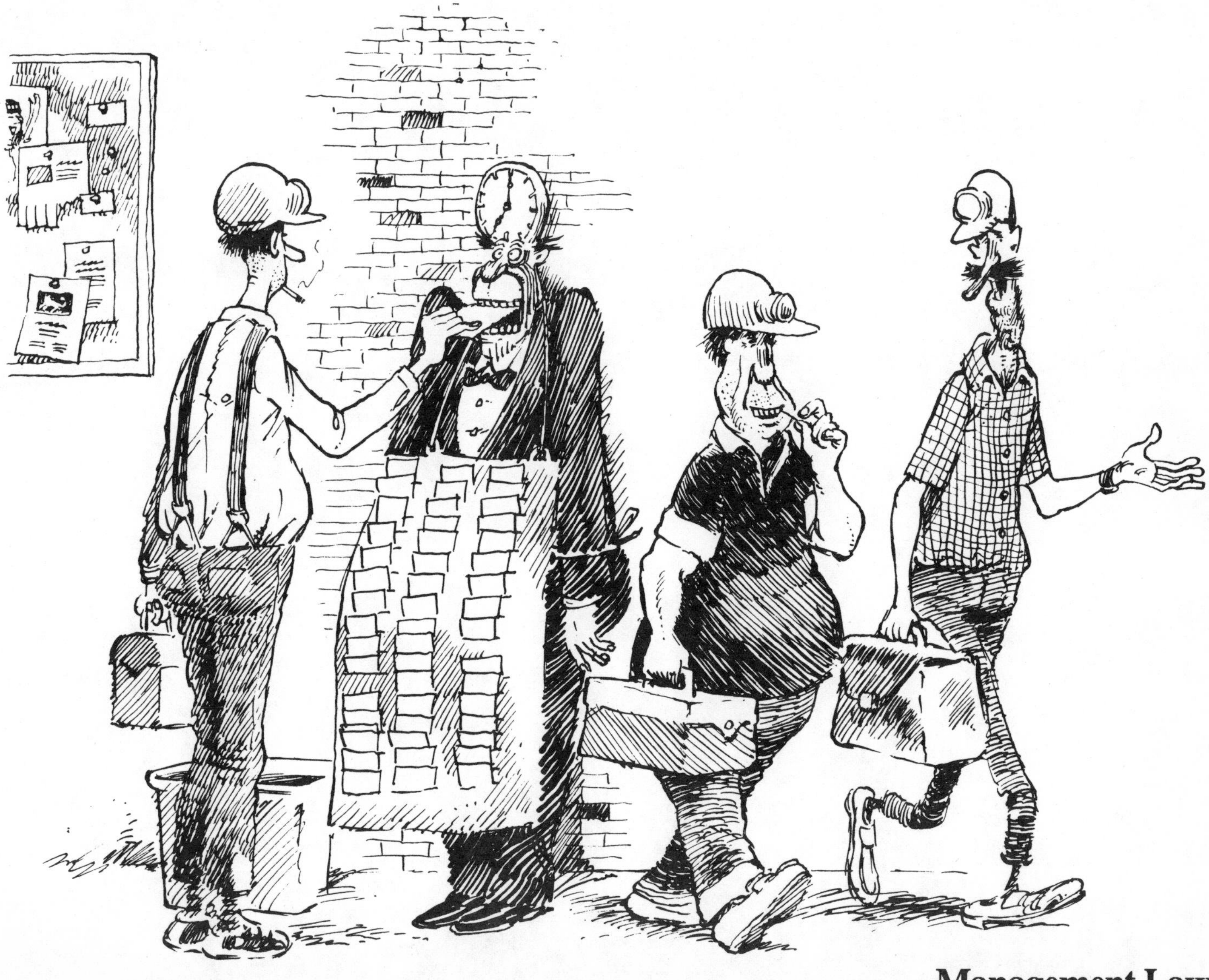

Management Lawyer

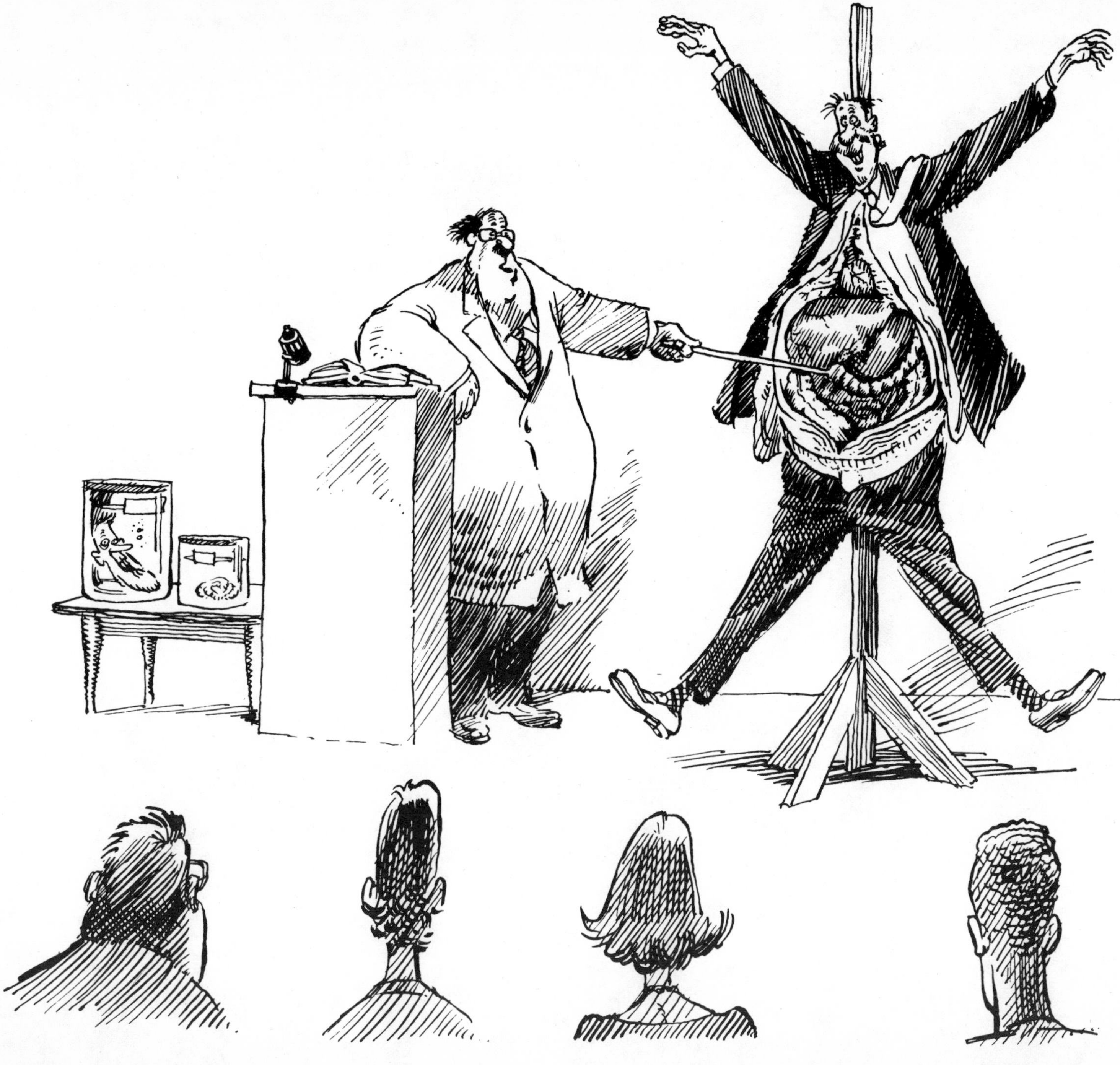

Medical Malpractice Lawyer

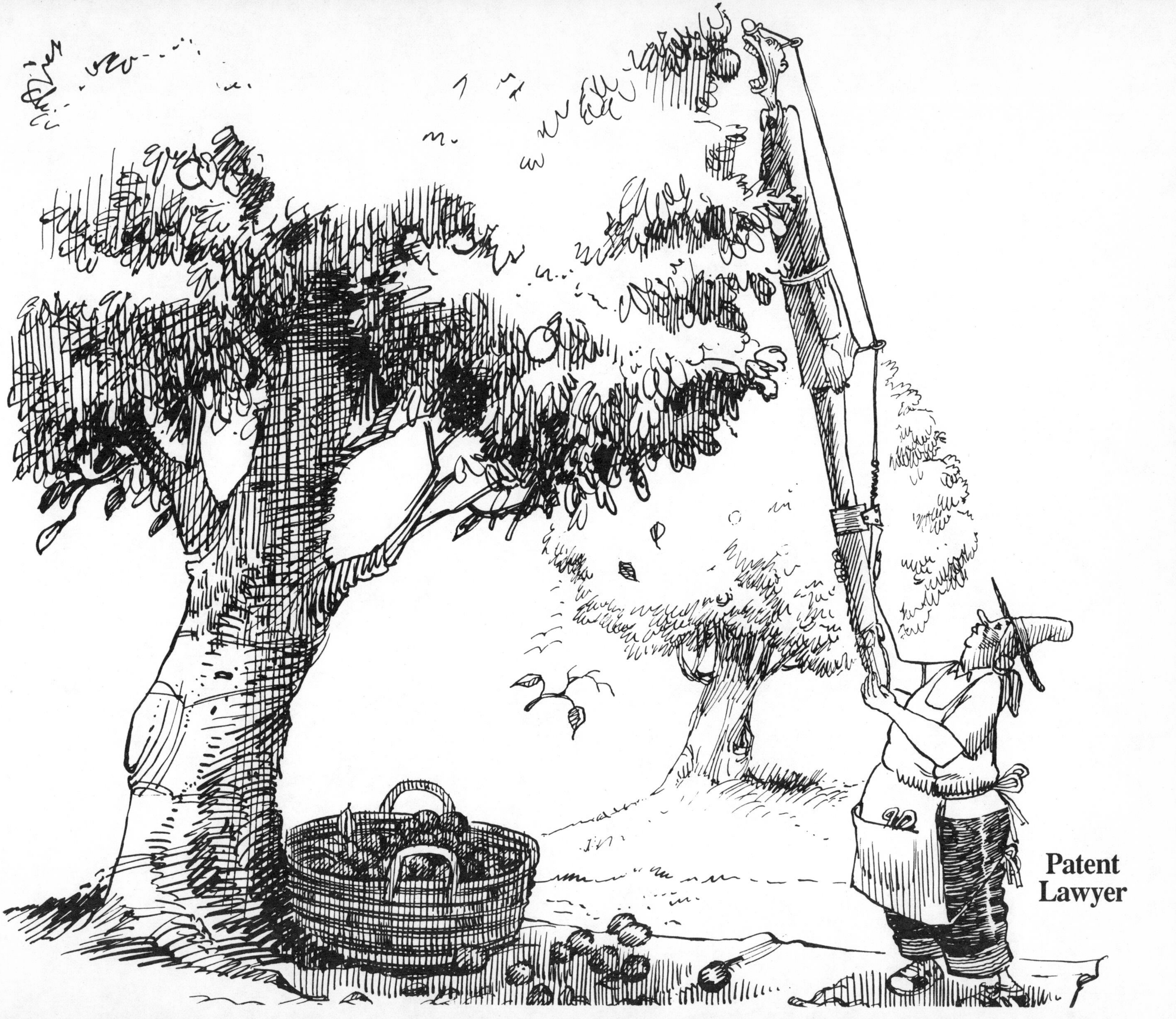

Patent Lawyer

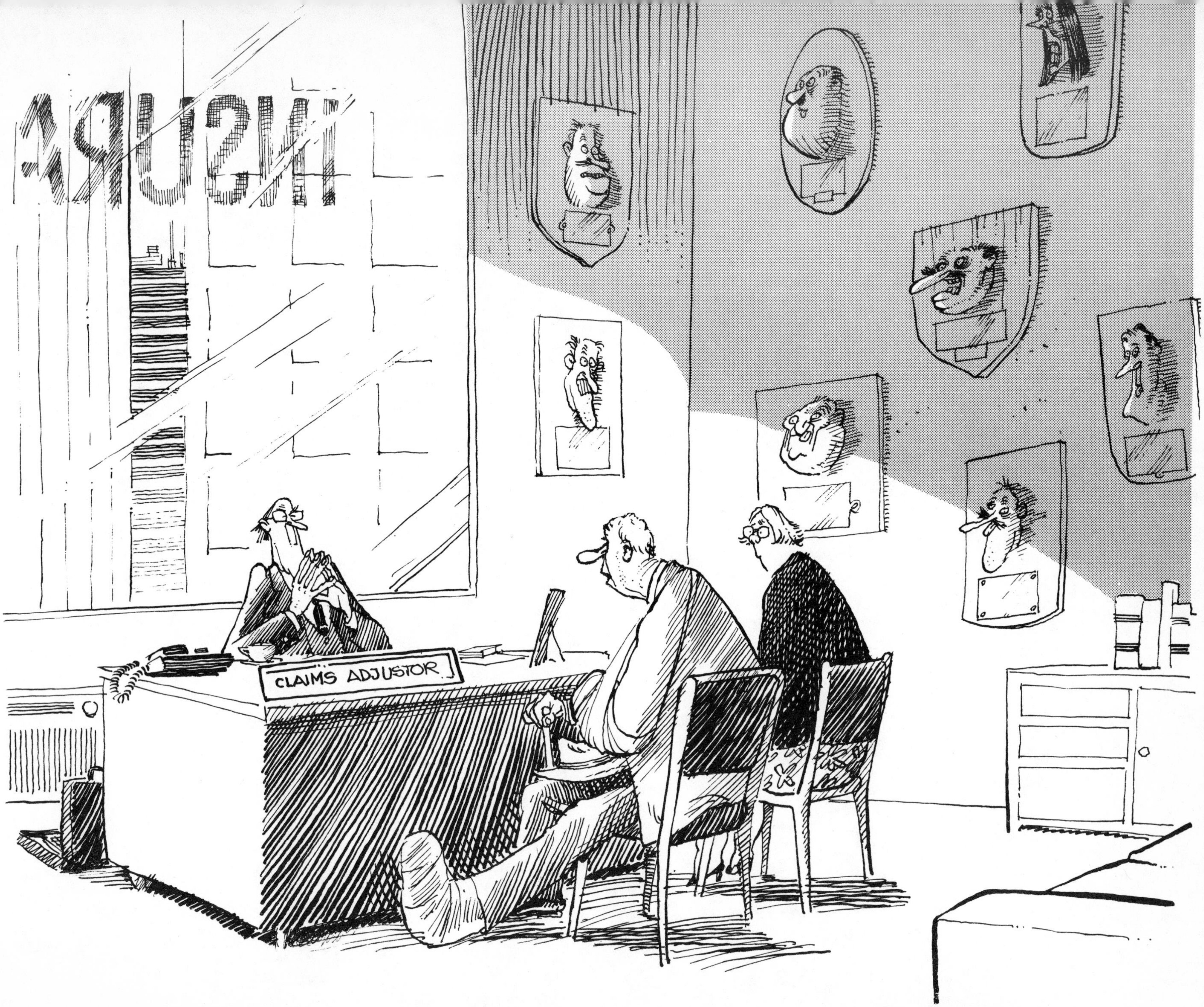

INSURA
CLAIMS ADJUSTOR

Personal Injury Lawyers

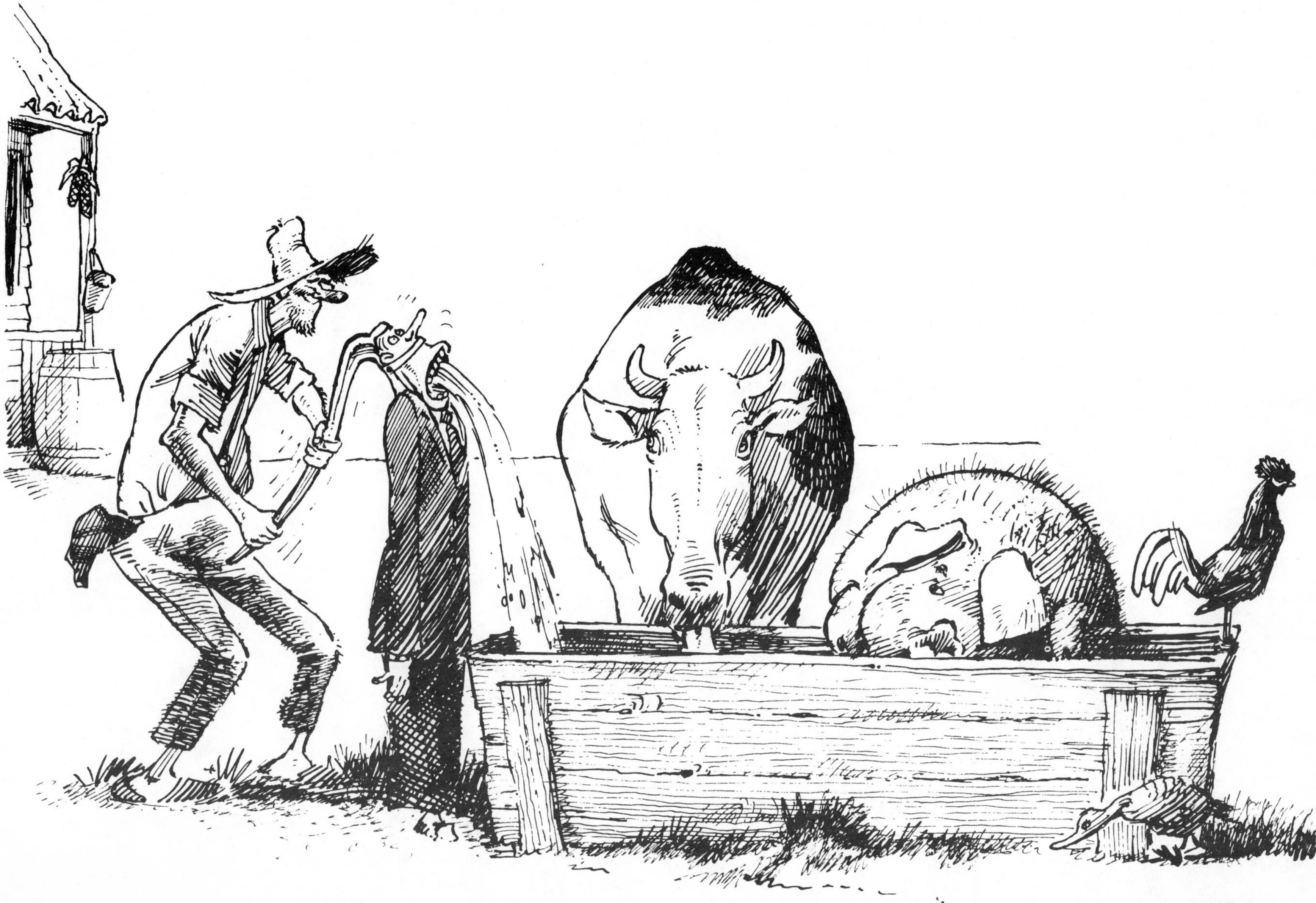

Philadelphia Lawyer

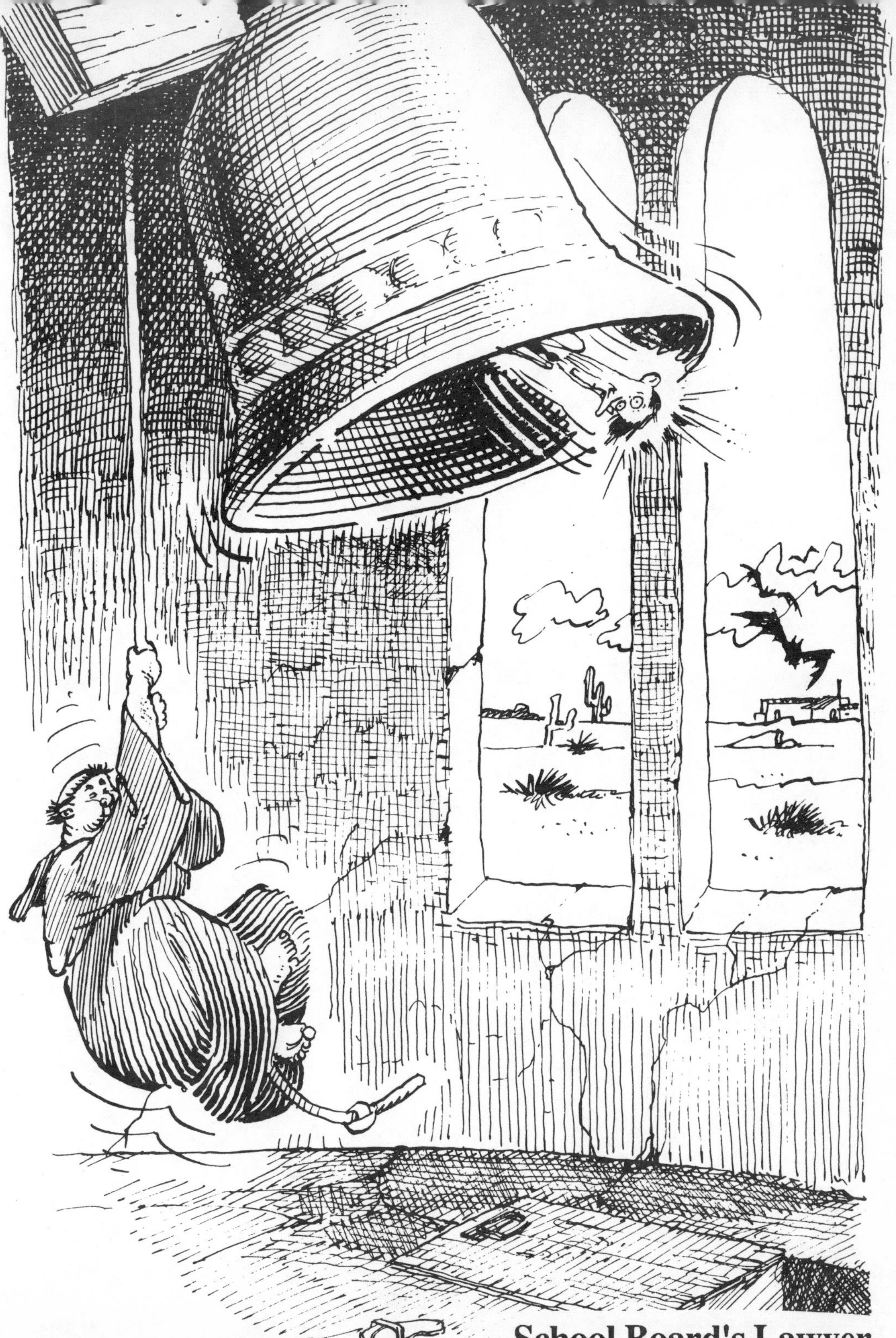

School Board's Lawyer

Securities Lawyer

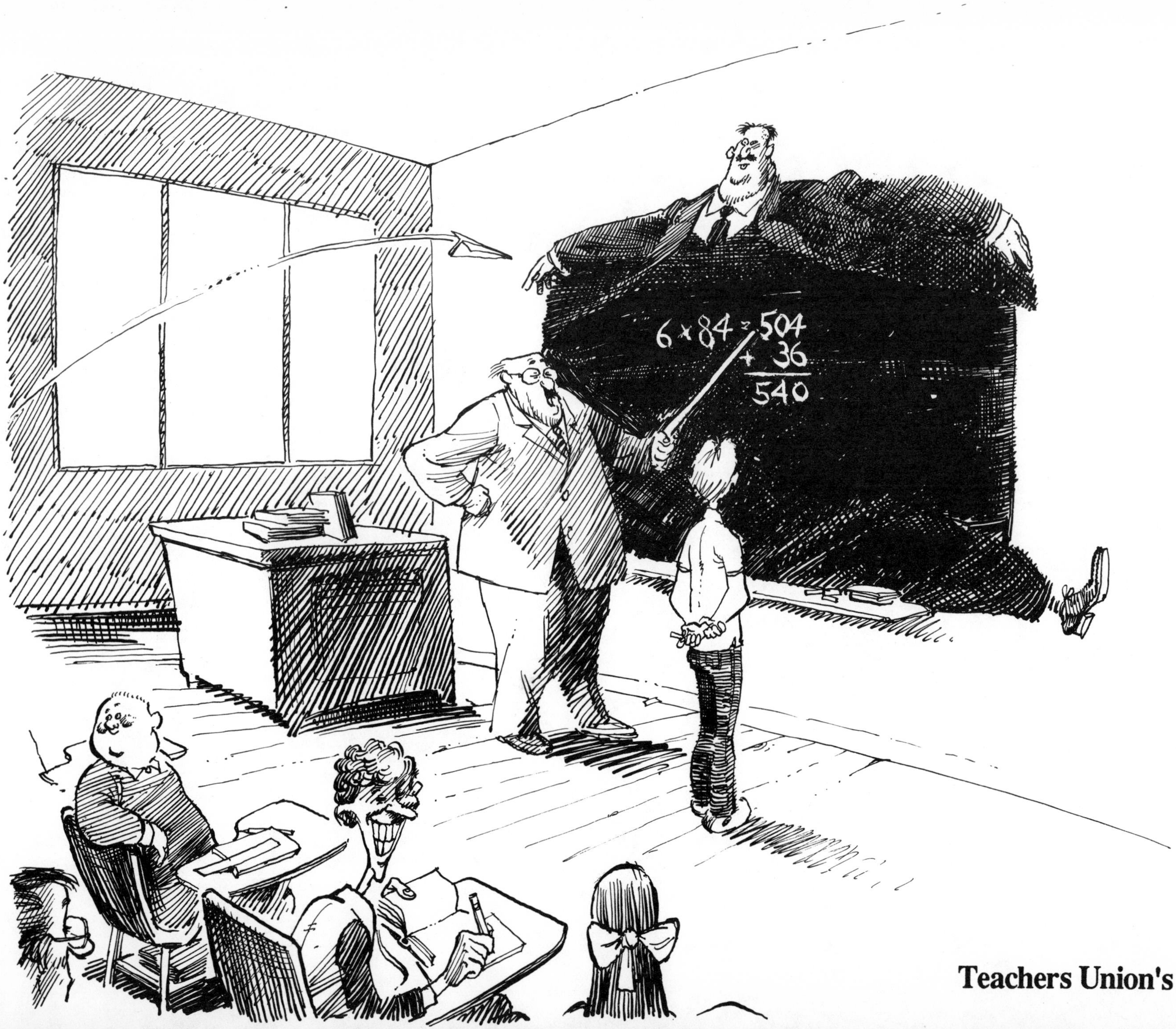
6 × 84 = 504
+ 36
540

Teachers Union's Lawyer

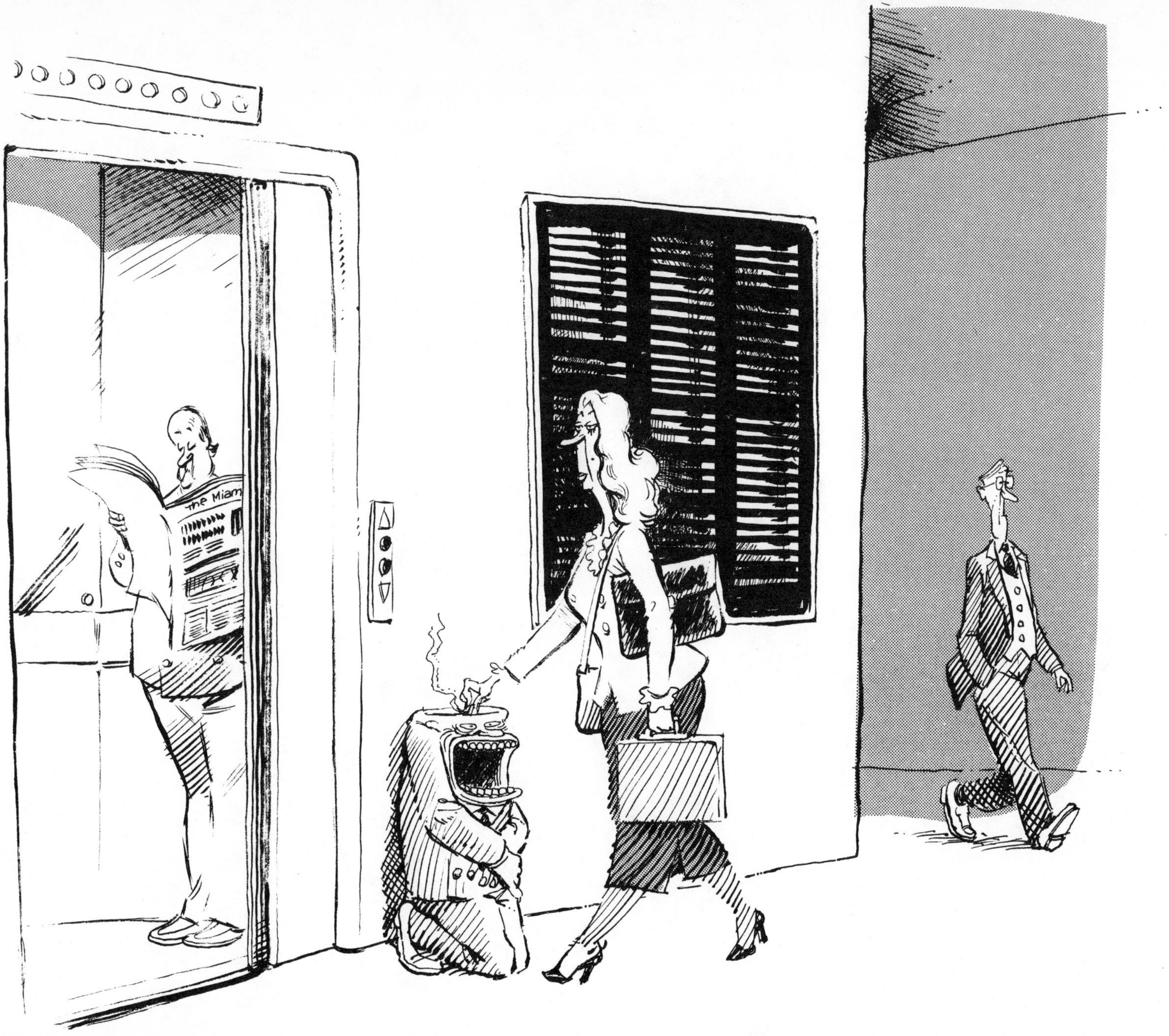
the Miam

Tobacco Company's Lawyer

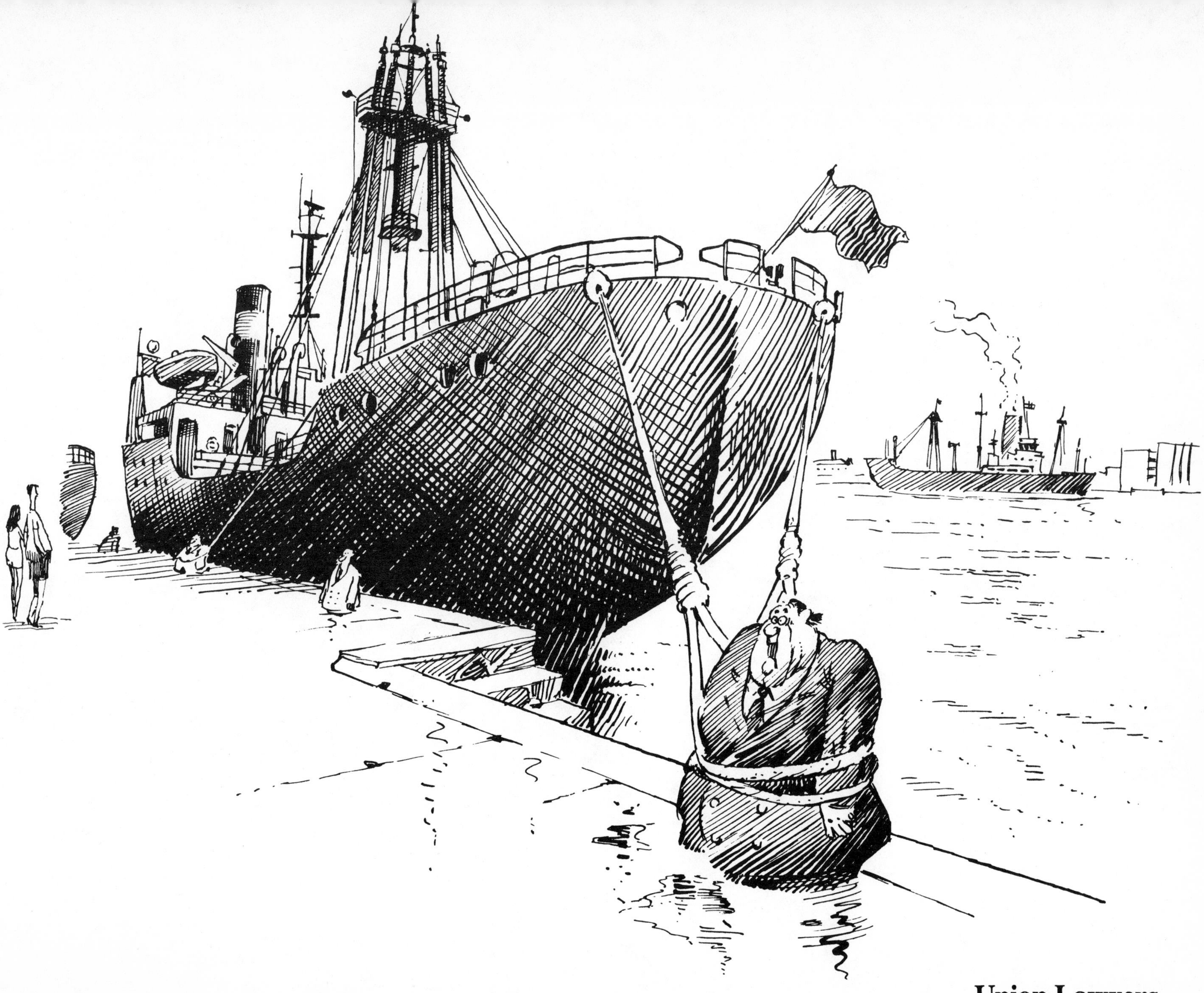

Union Lawyers

At play

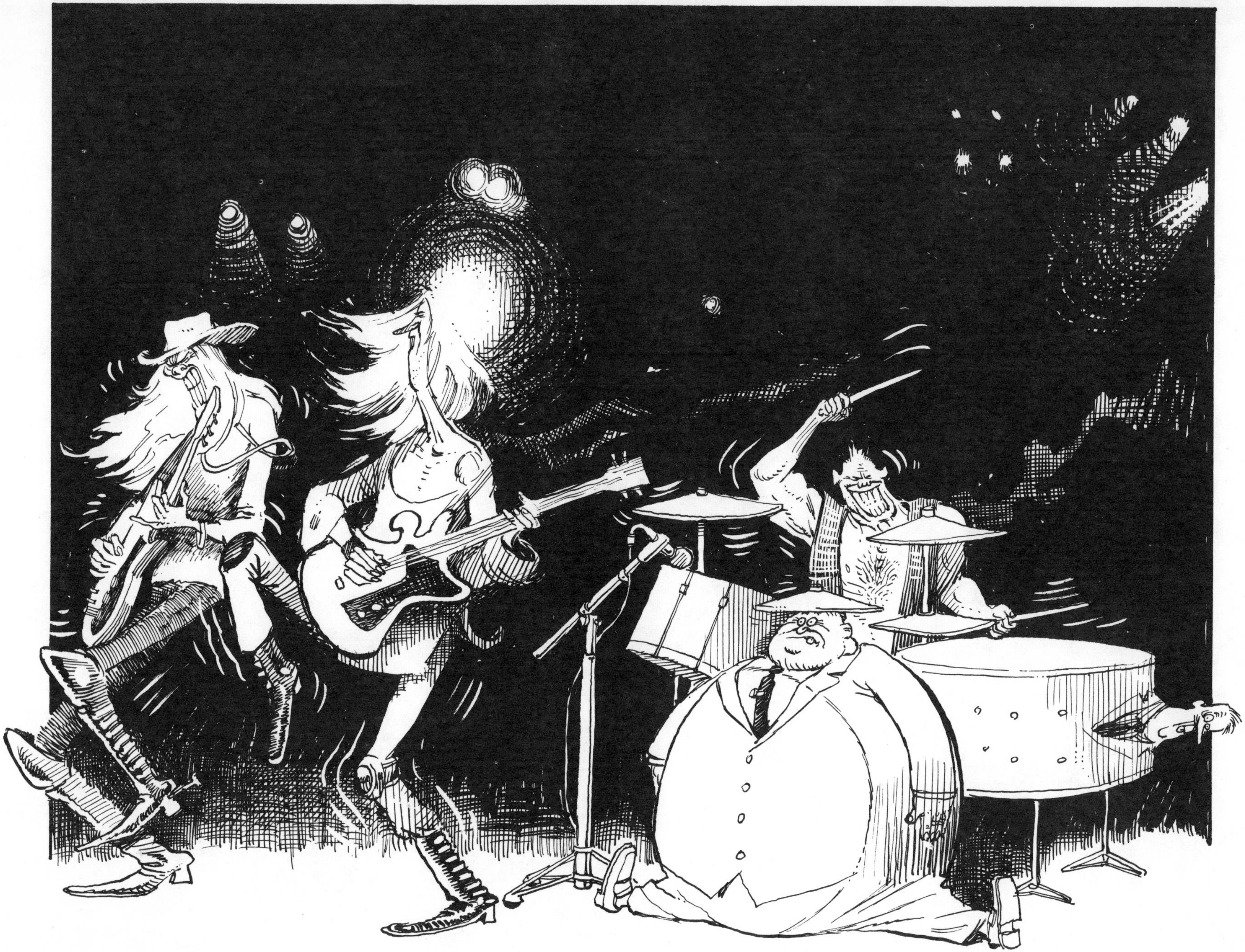

Censorship Lawyers

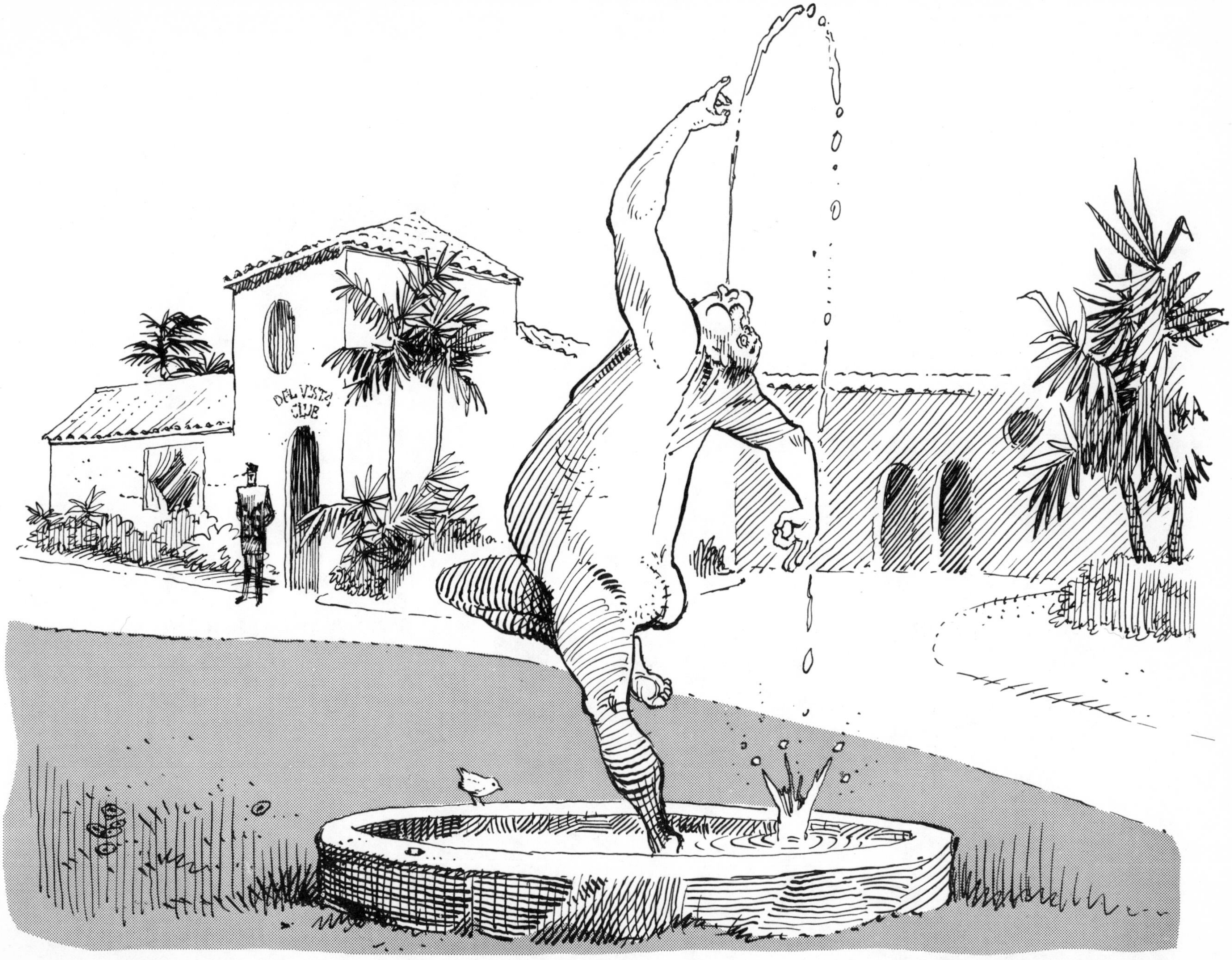
DEL VISTA
CLUB

Country Club's Lawyer

Custody Lawyer

Entertainment Lawyer

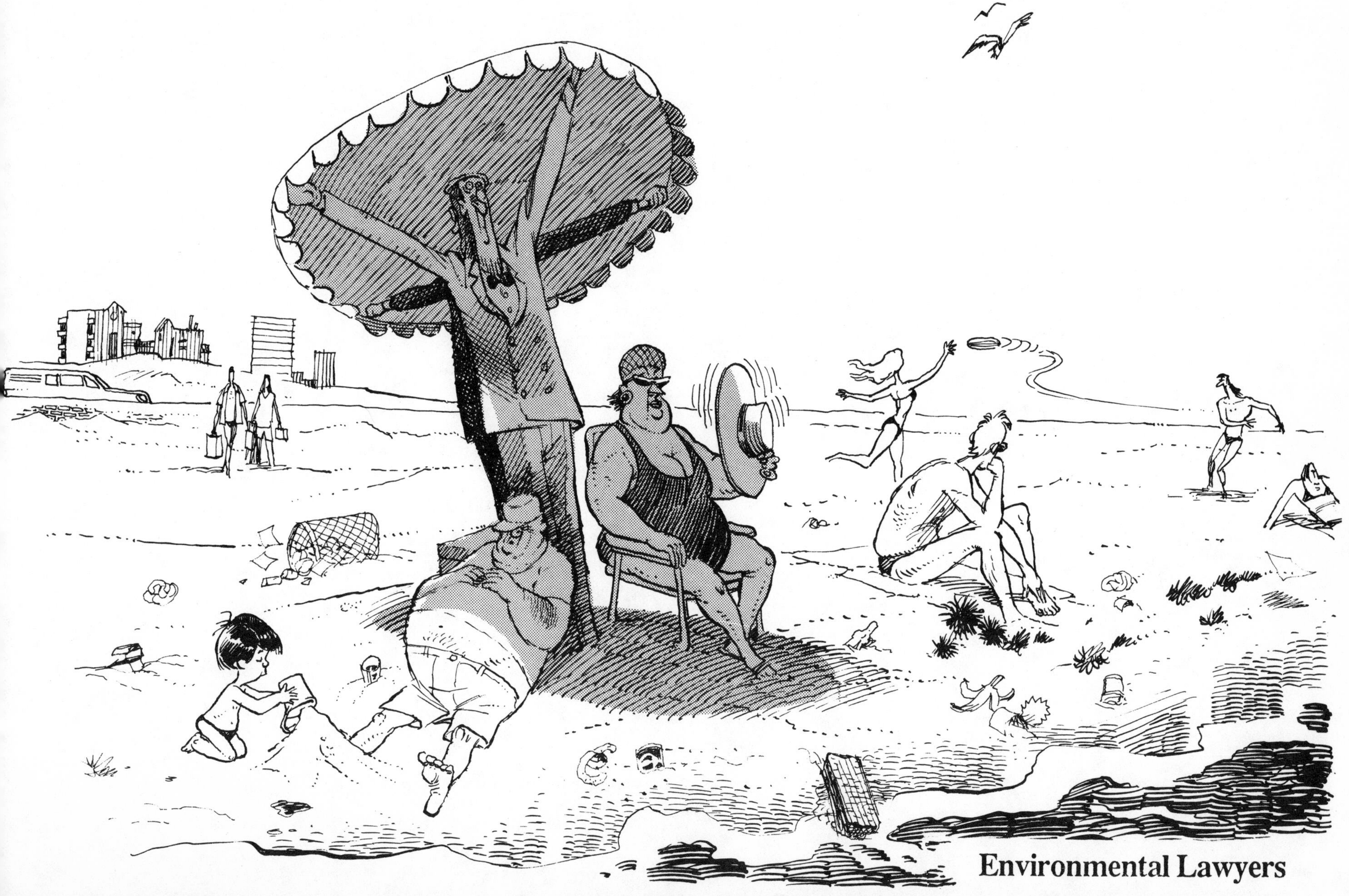

Environmental Lawyers

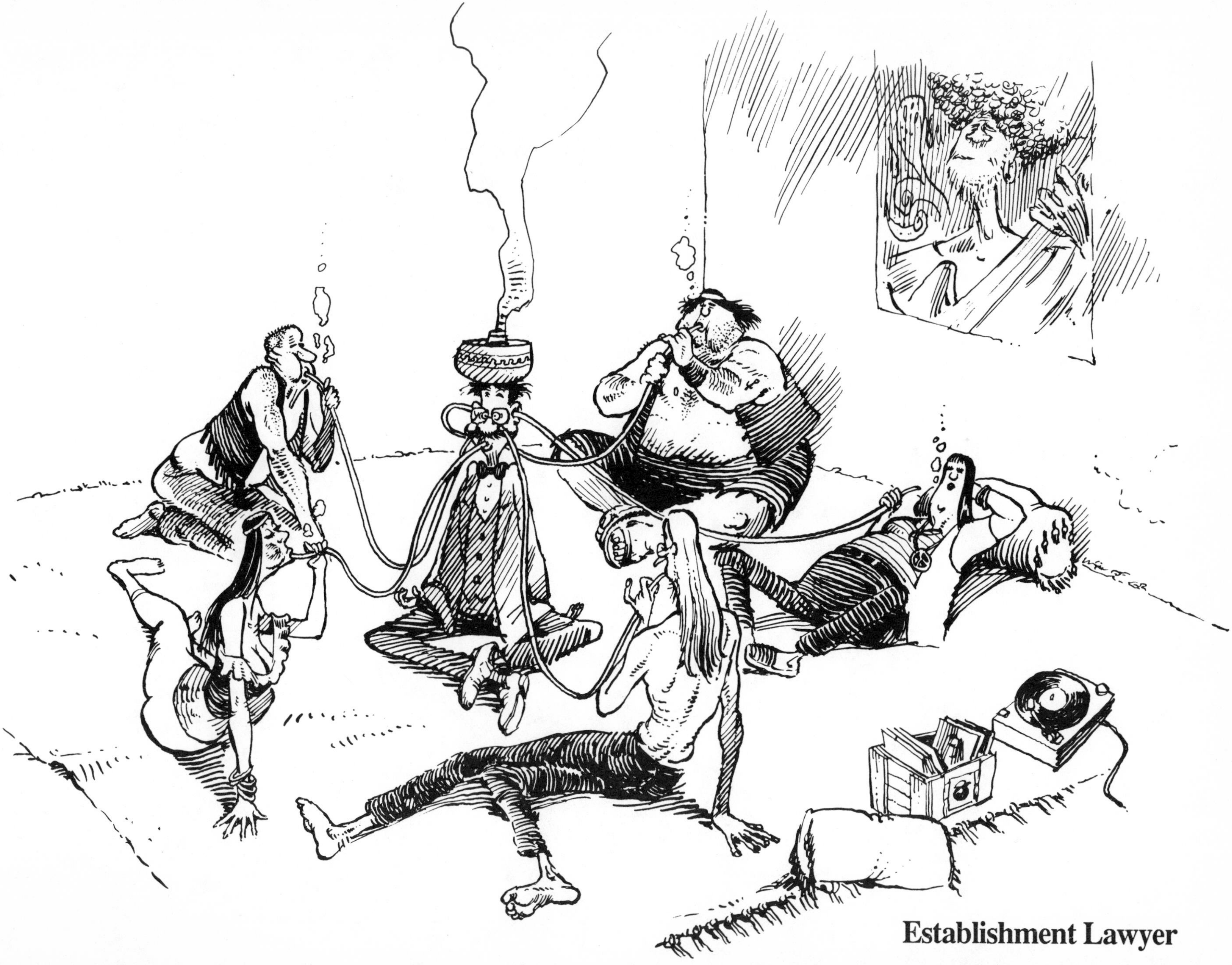

Establishment Lawyer

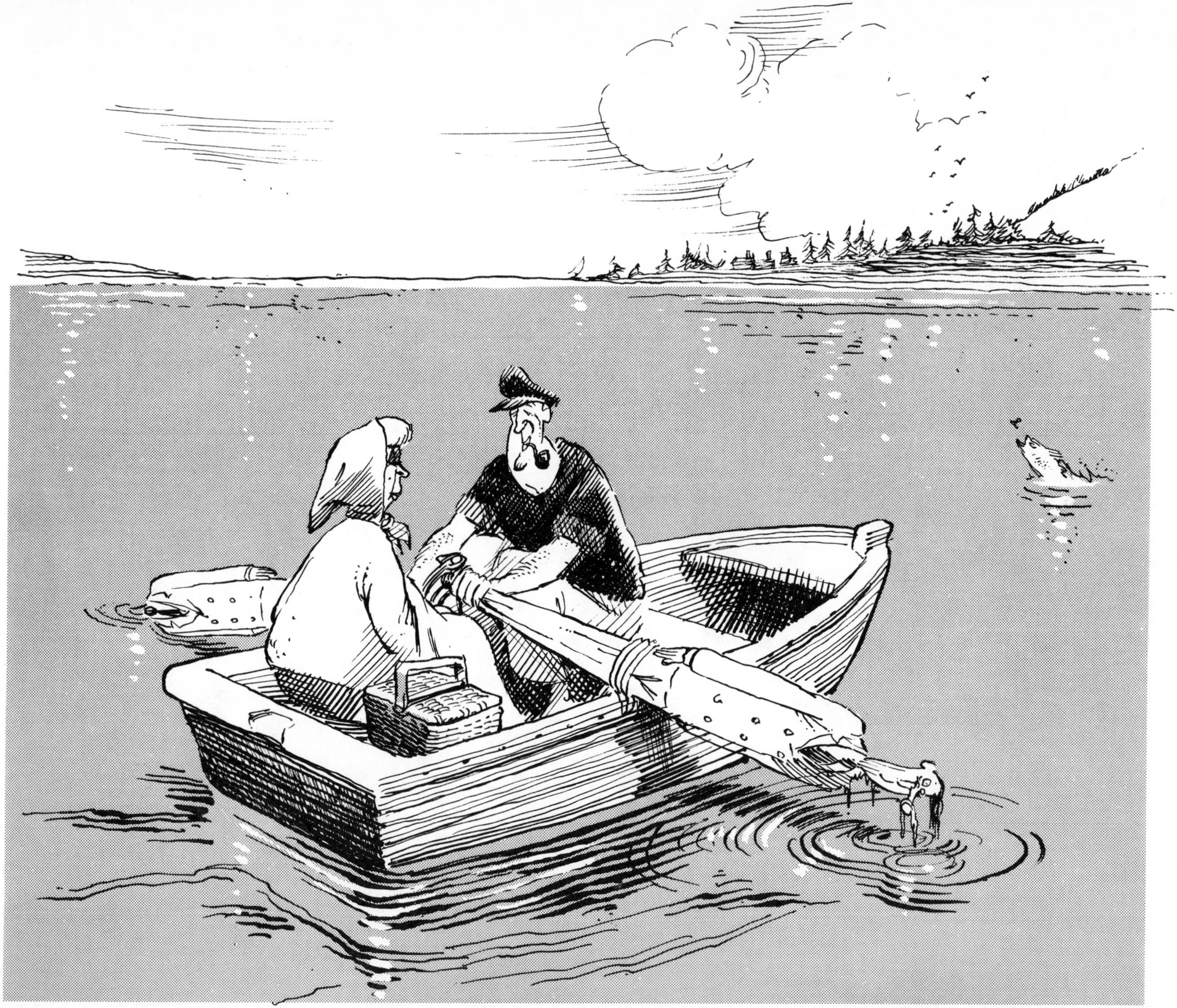

Estate Planning Lawyers

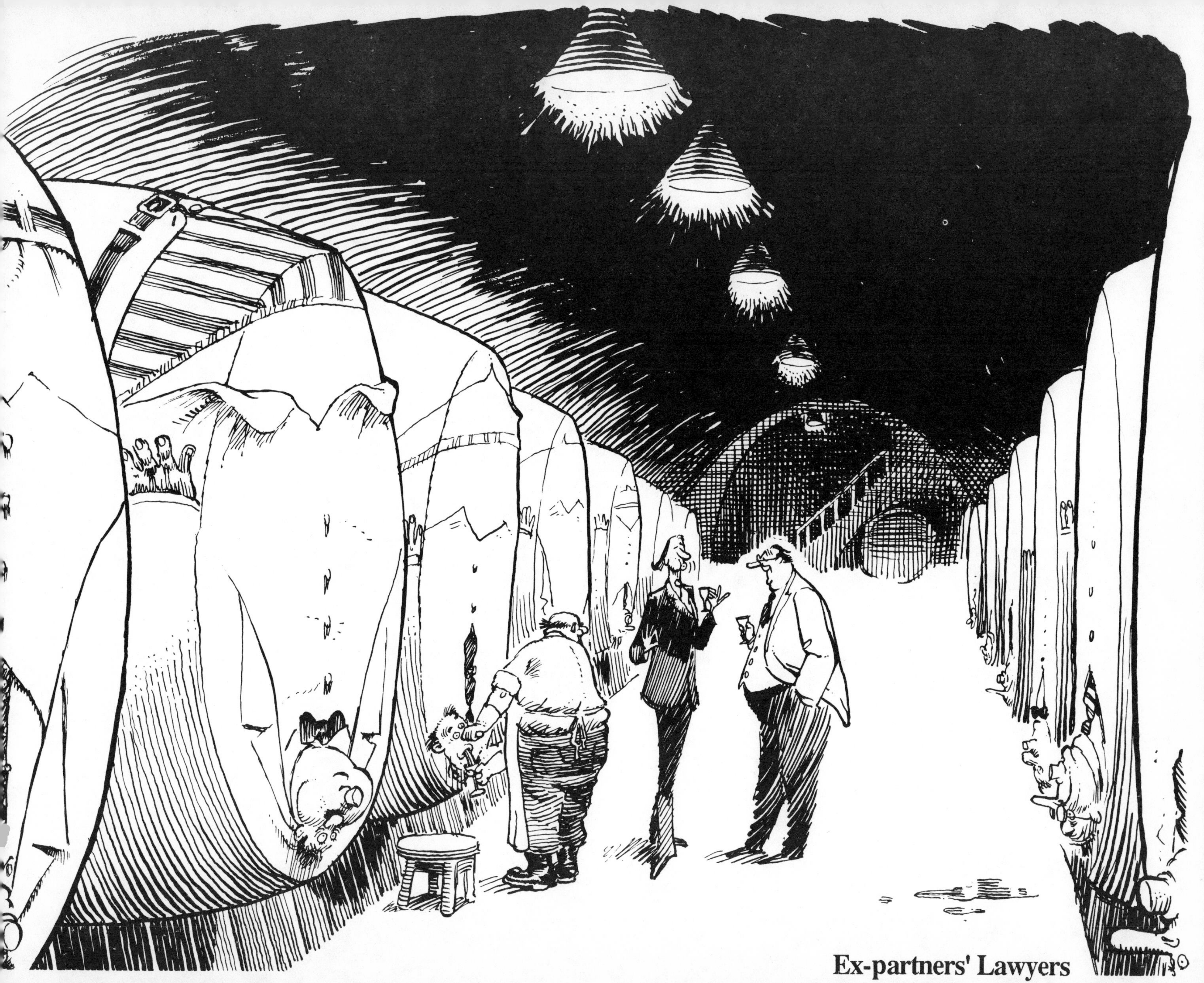

Ex-partners' Lawyers

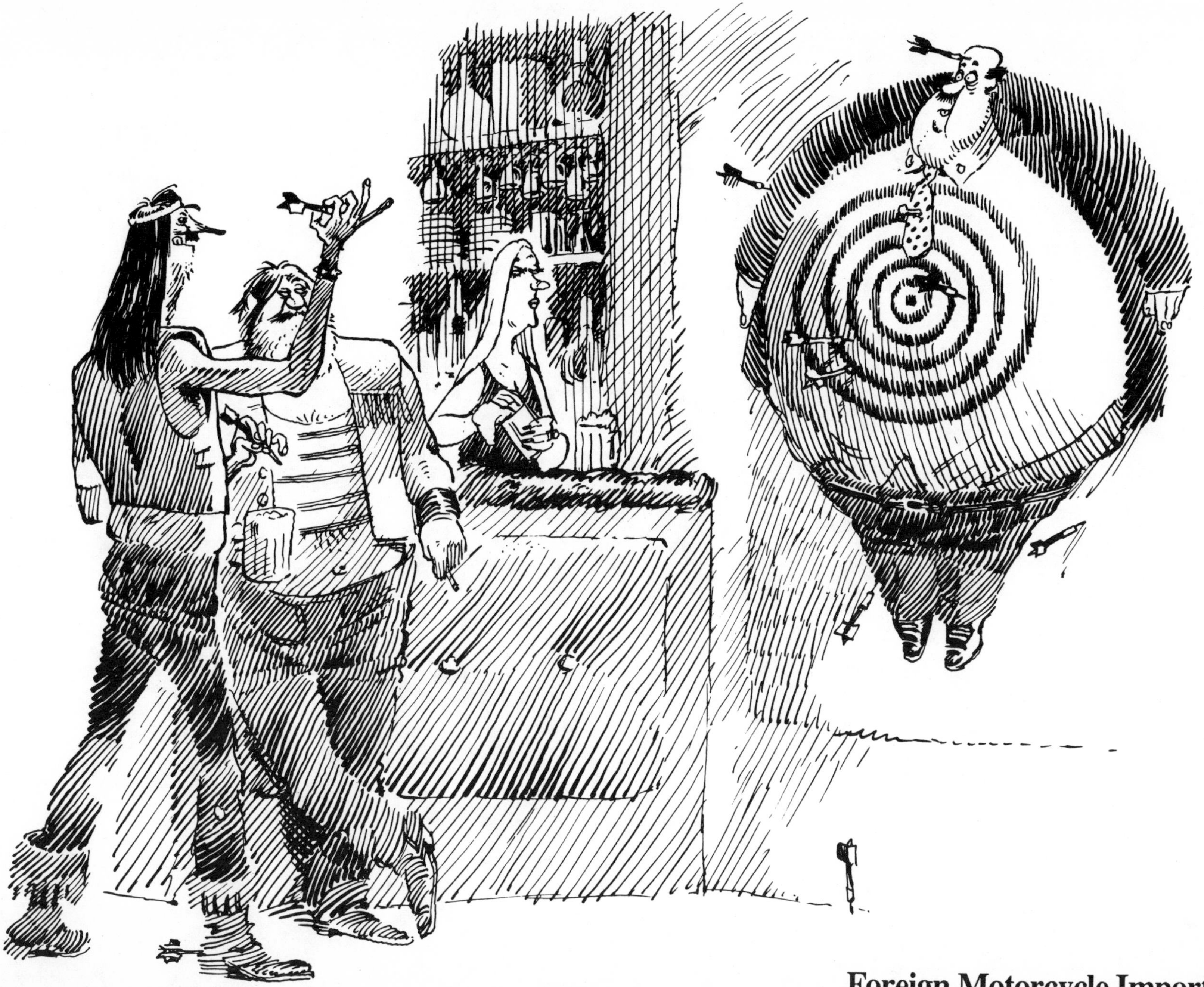

Foreign Motorcycle Importer's Lawyer

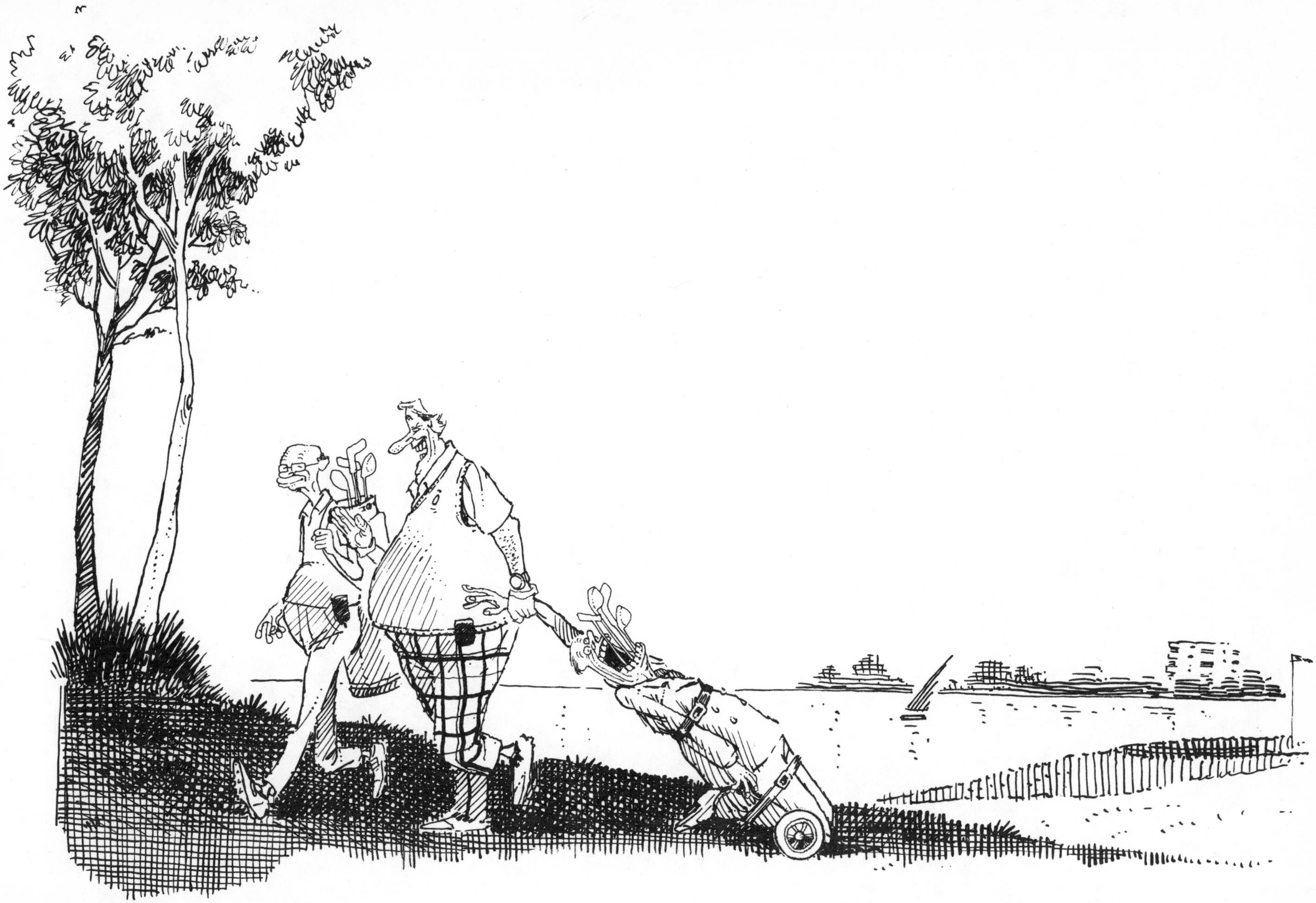

Medical Malpractice Lawyer

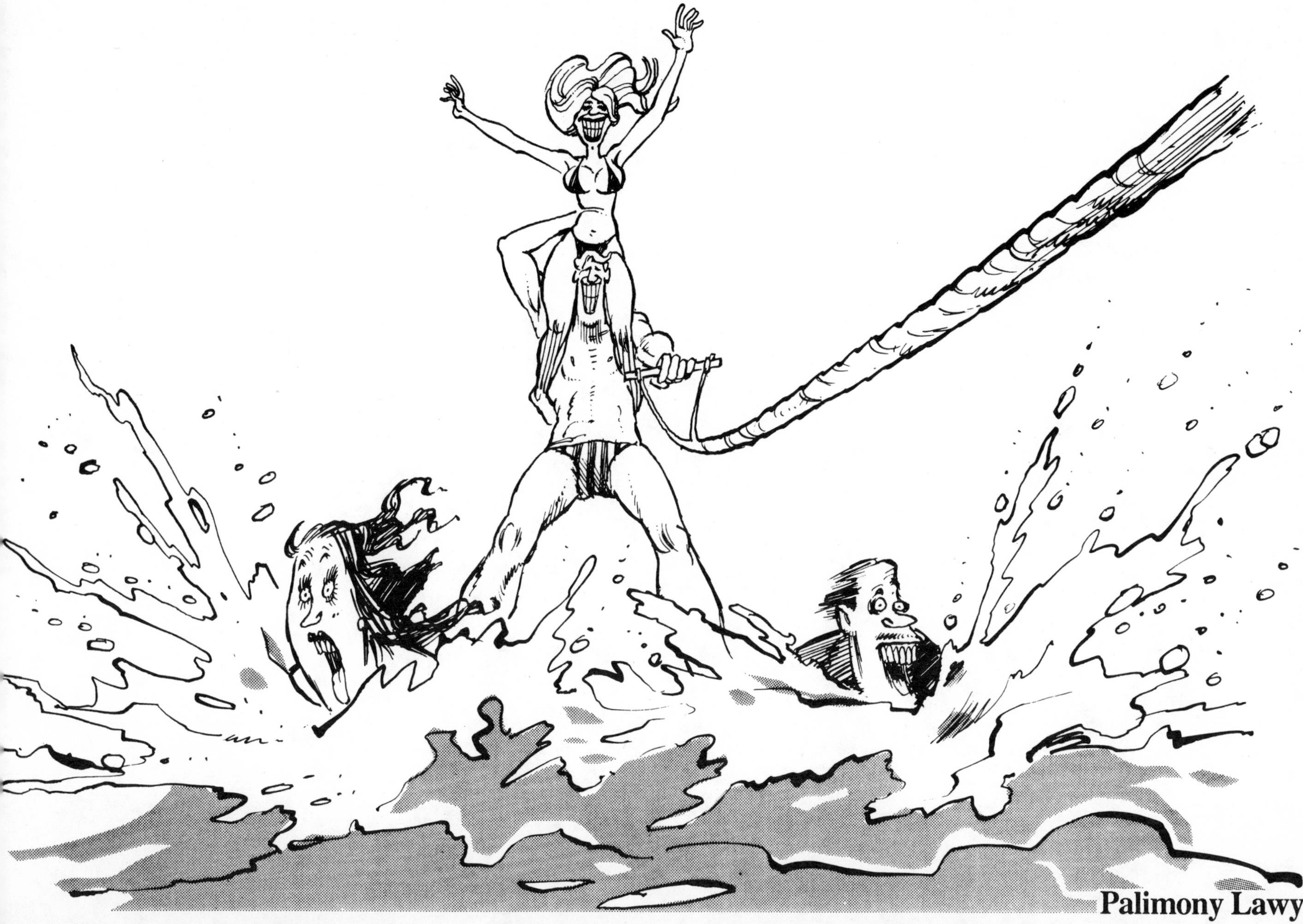

Palimony Lawyers

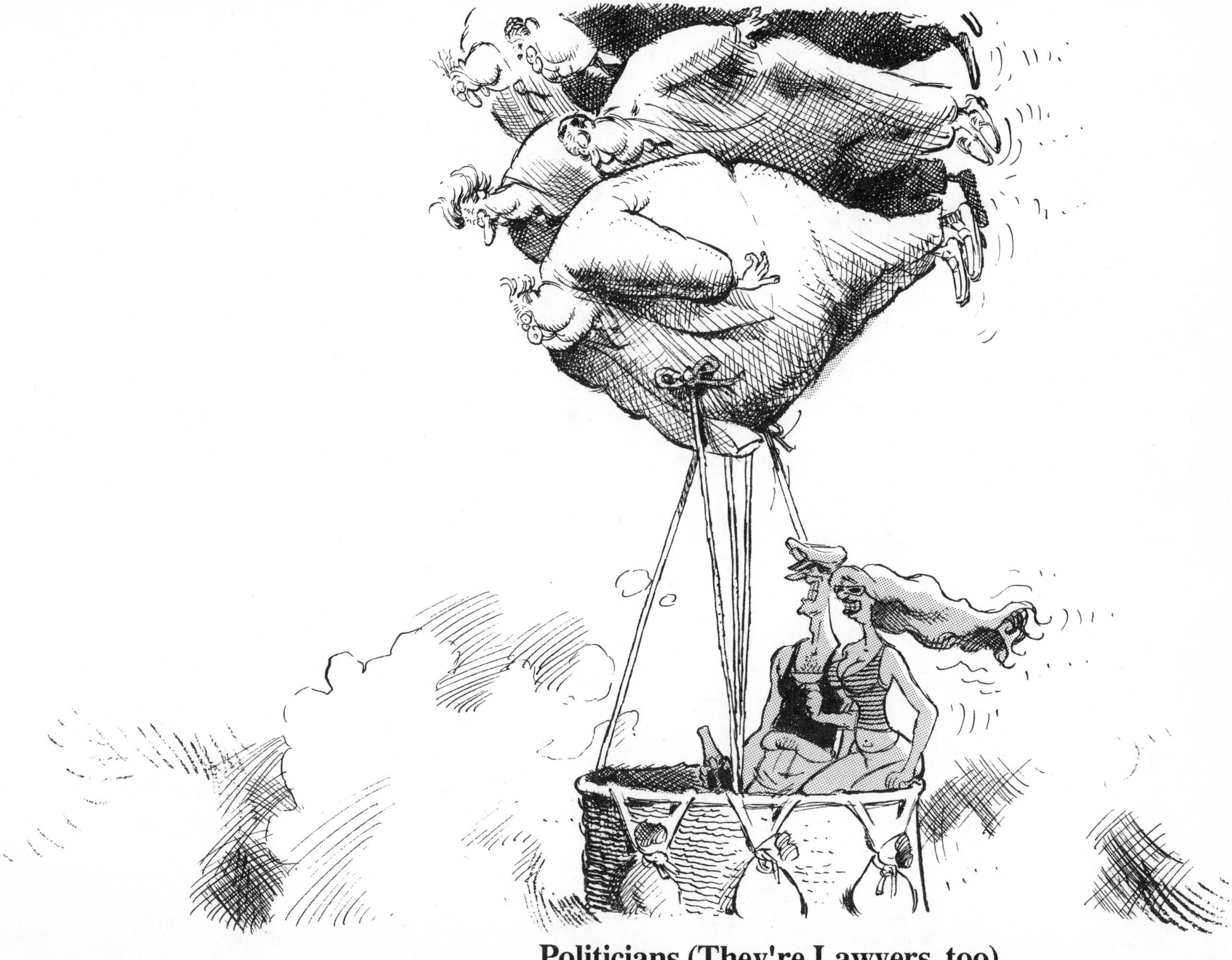

Politicians (They're Lawyers, too)

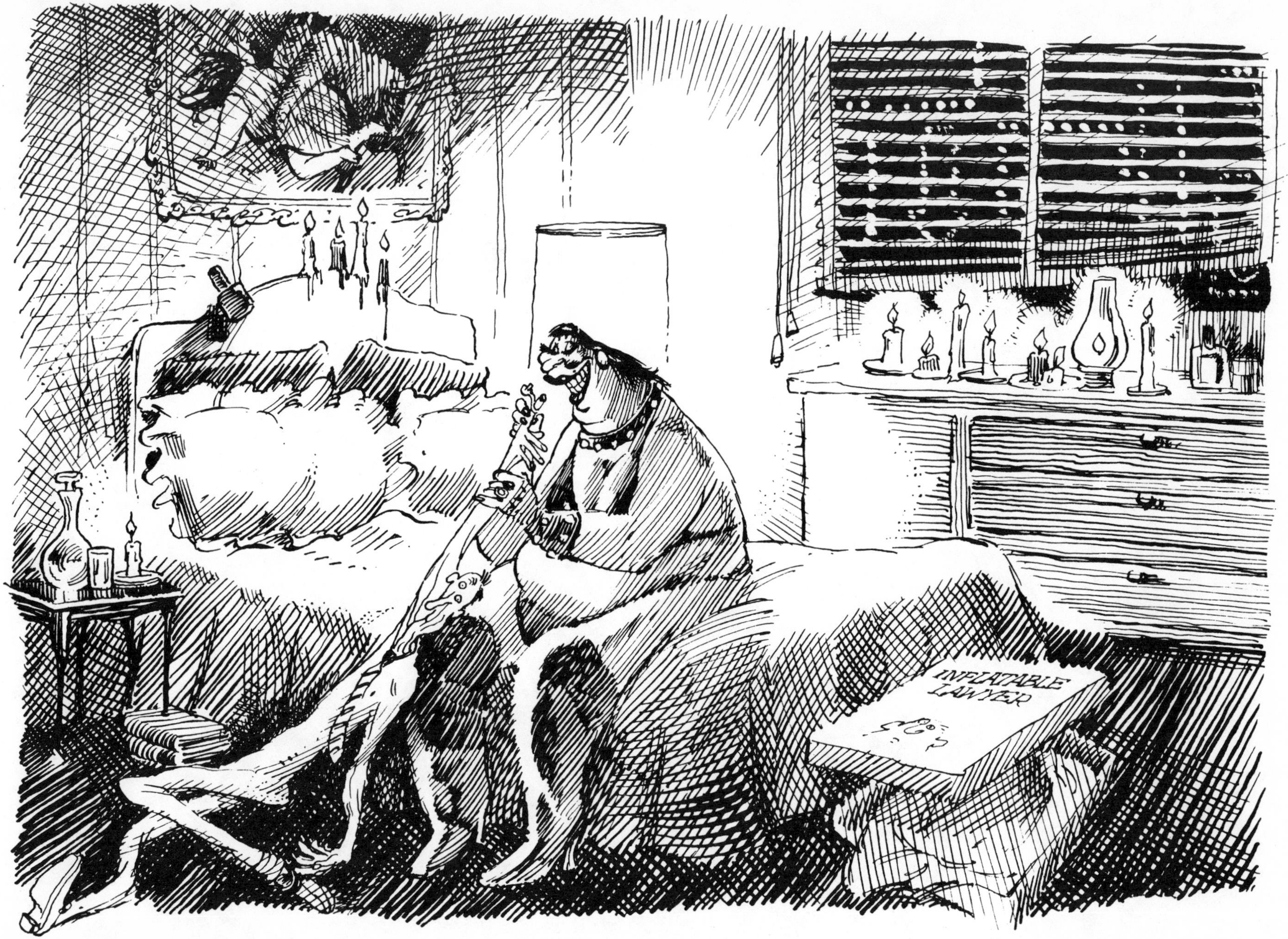
INFLATABLE
LAWYER

Porno Shop's Lawyer

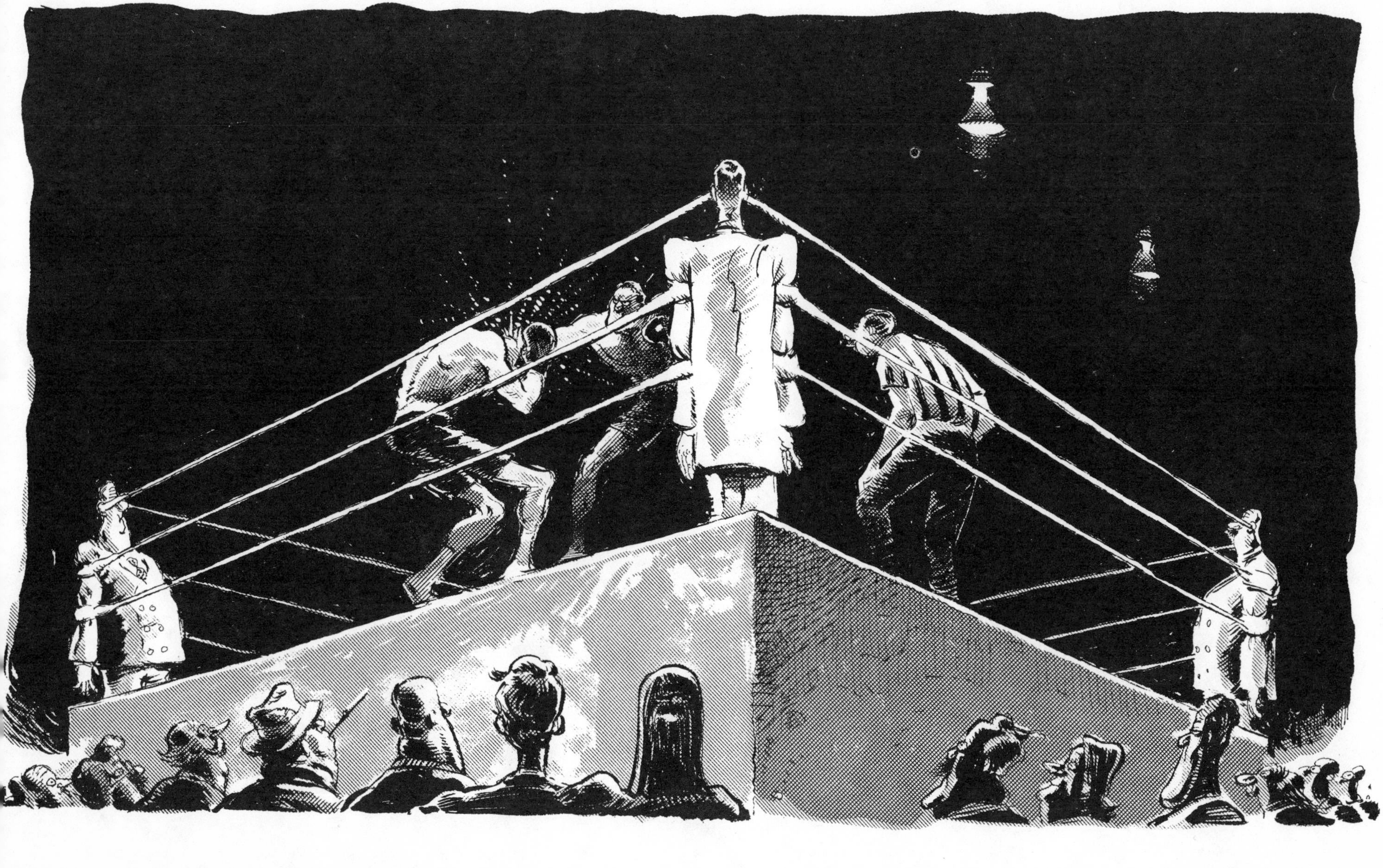

Sports Lawyers

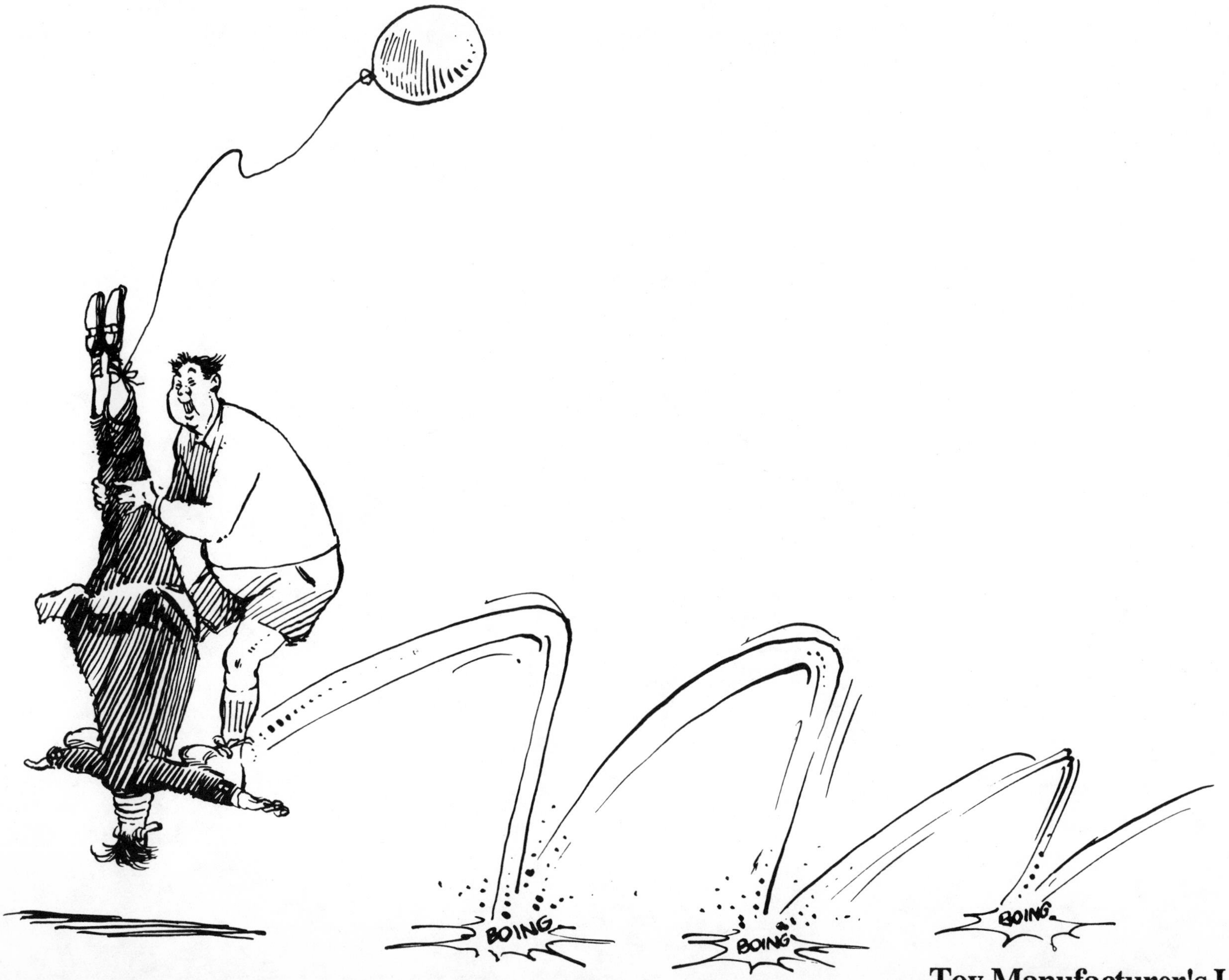
BOING
BOING
BOING

Toy Manufacturer's Lawyer

Yuppie Lawyer

On the go

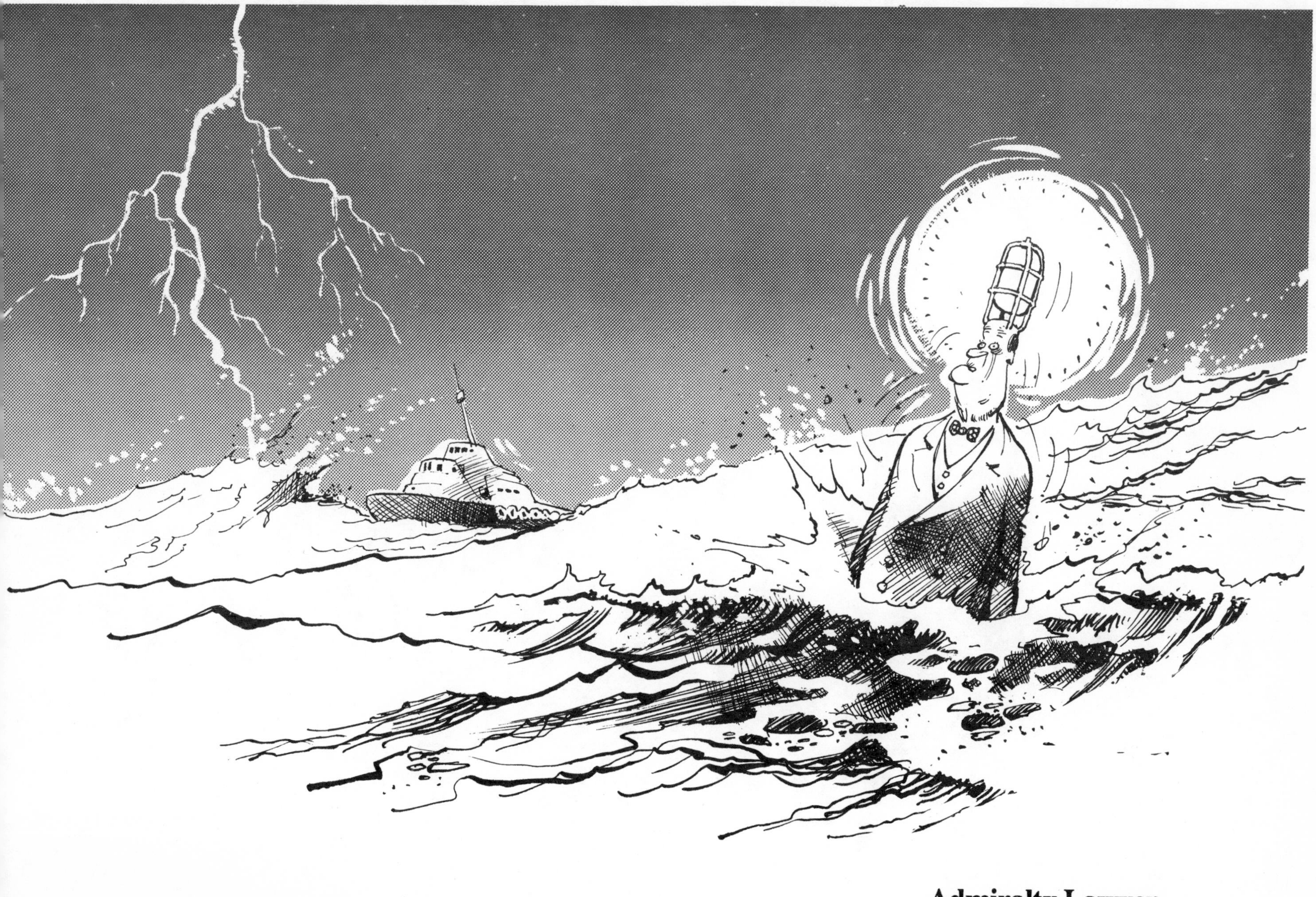

Admiralty Lawyer

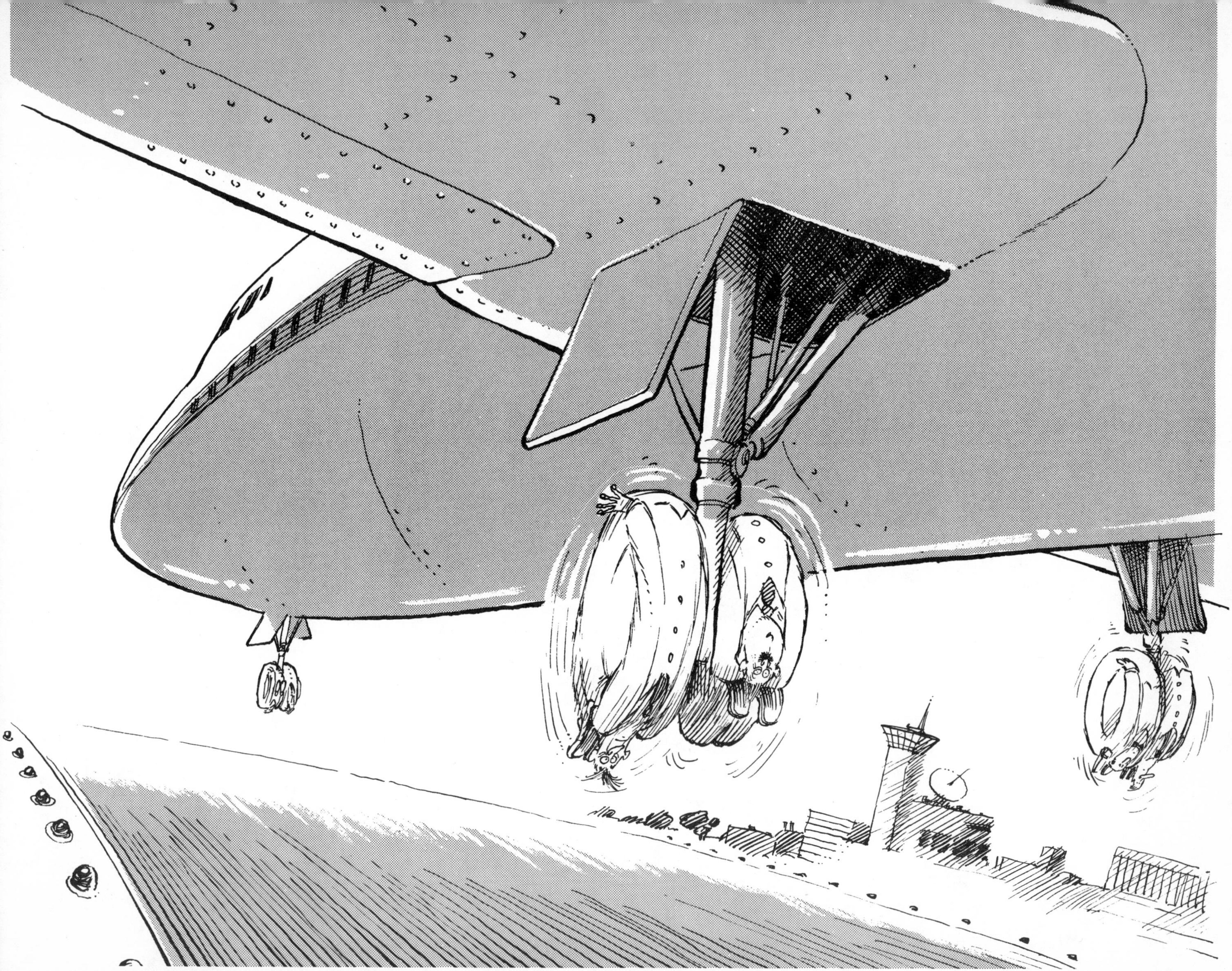

Airlines' Lawyers

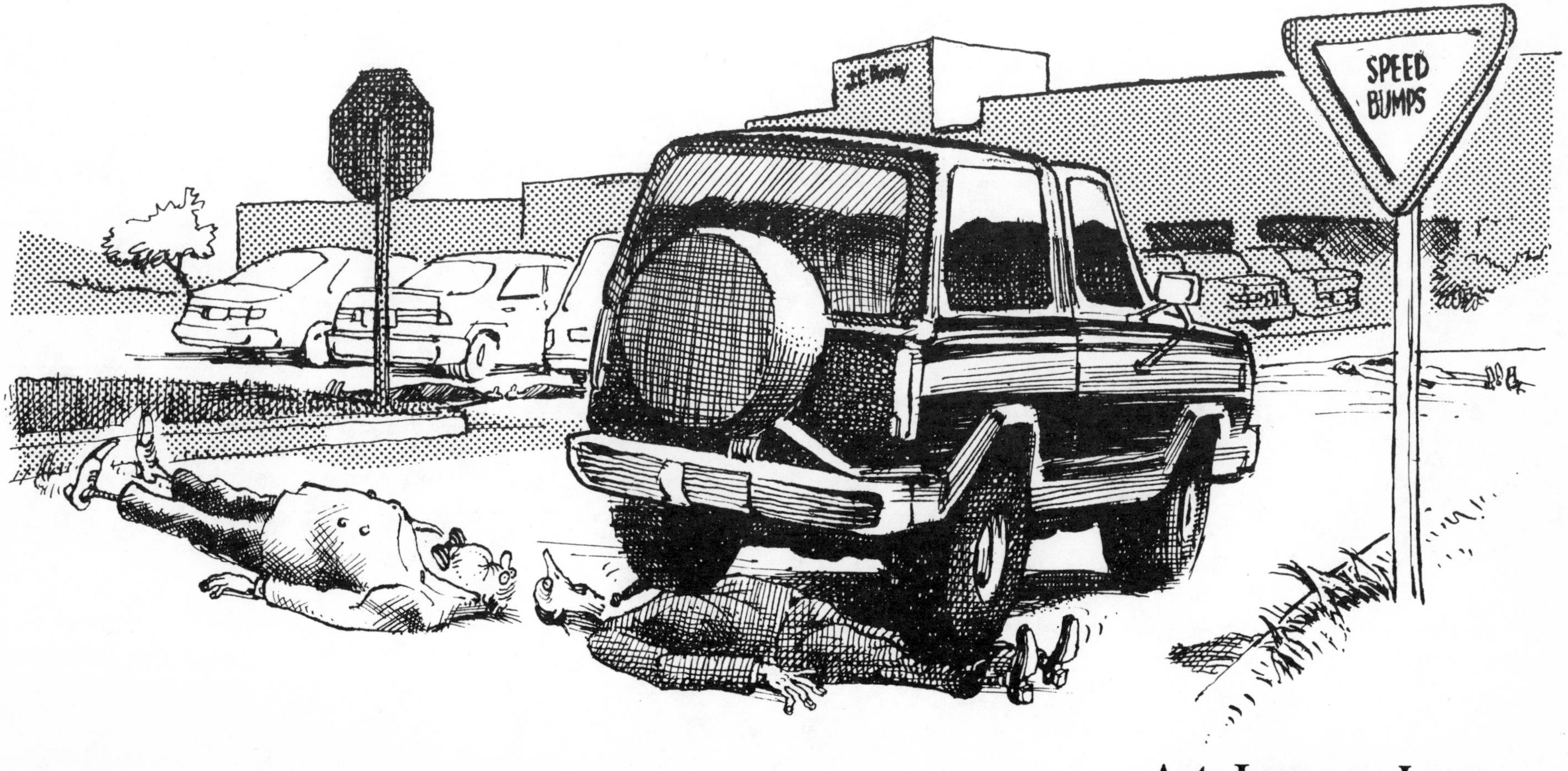
SPEED
BUMPS

Auto Insurance Lawyers

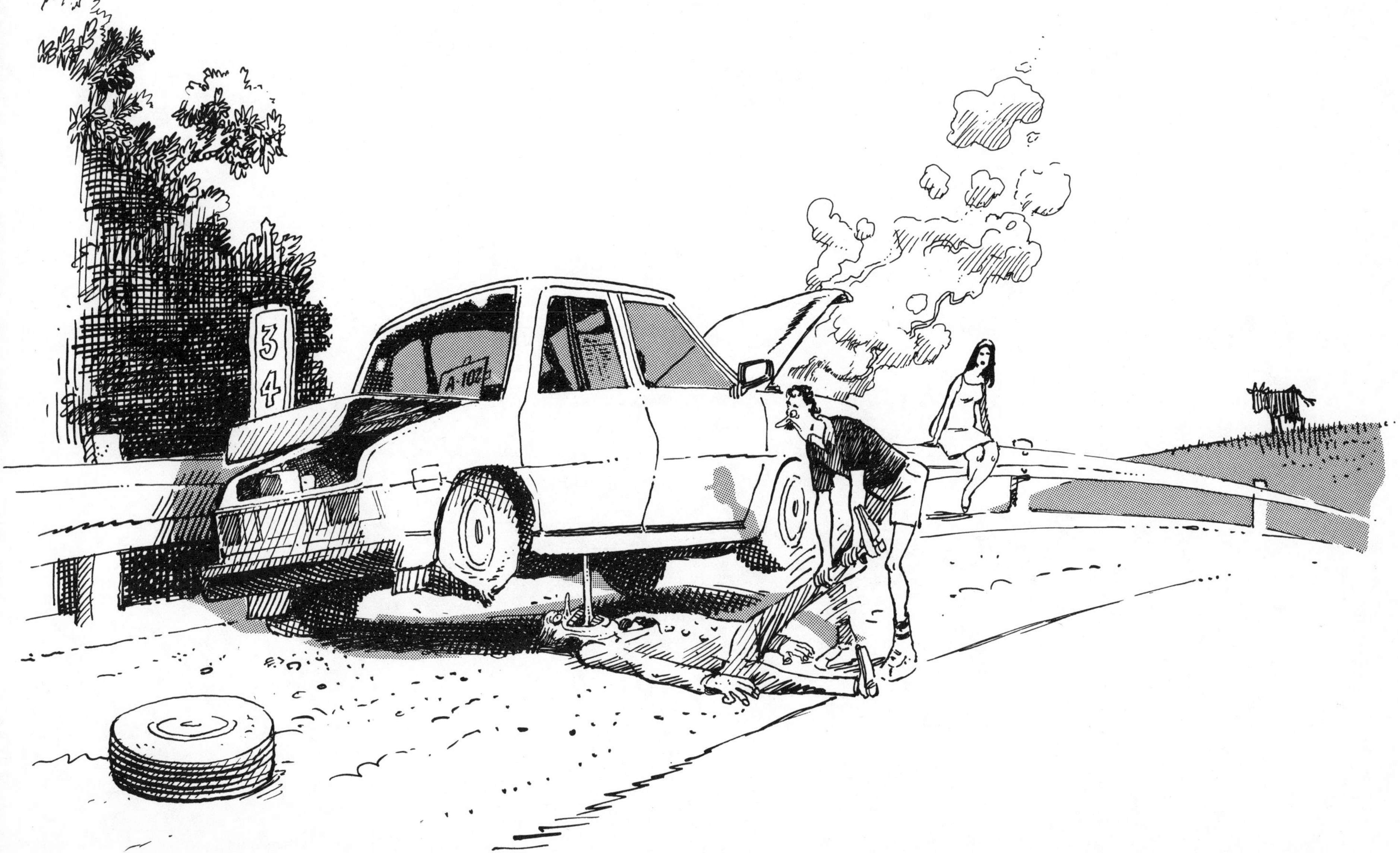
3
4
A-102

Car Dealer's Lawyer

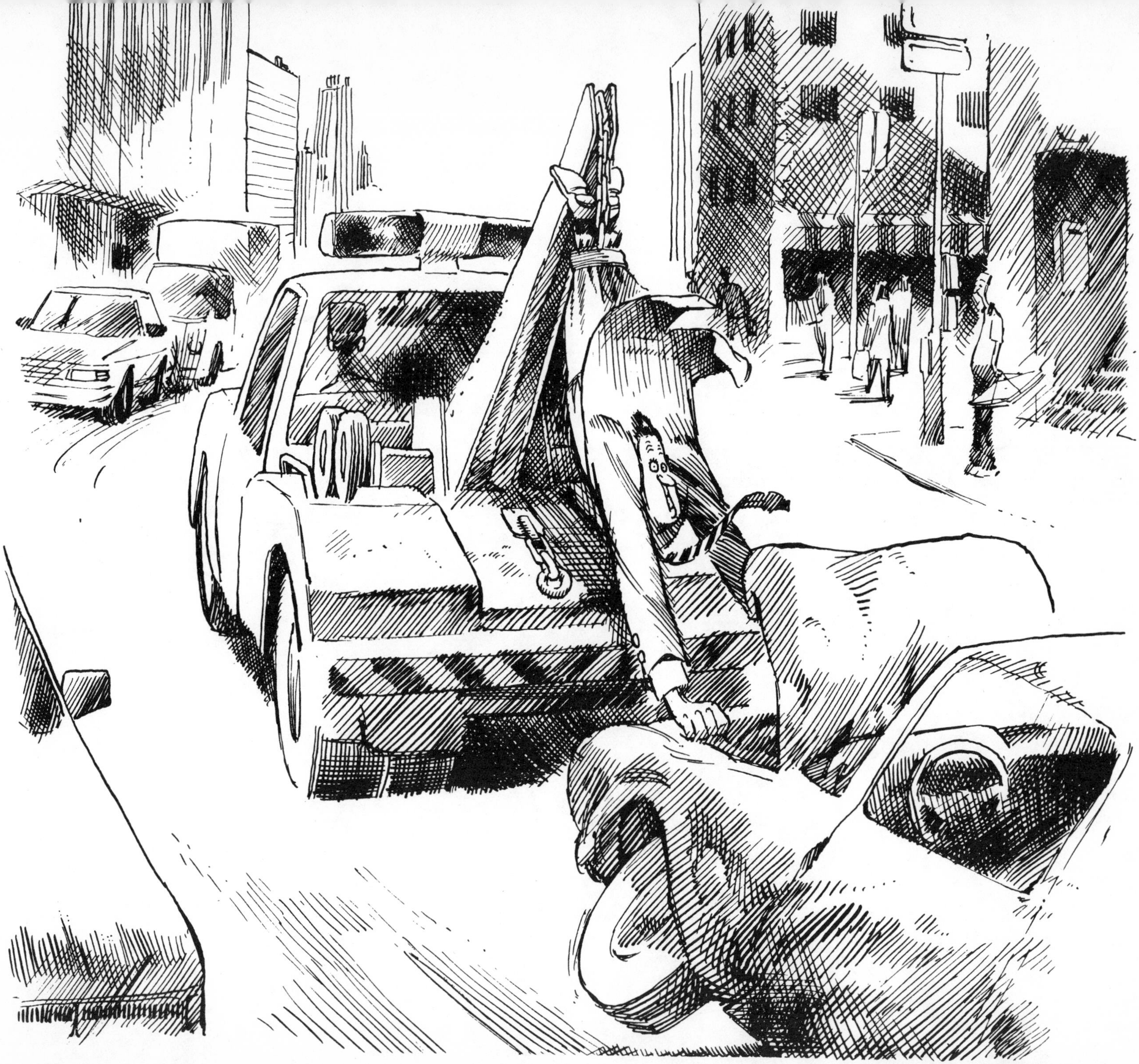

Car Mechanic's Lawyer

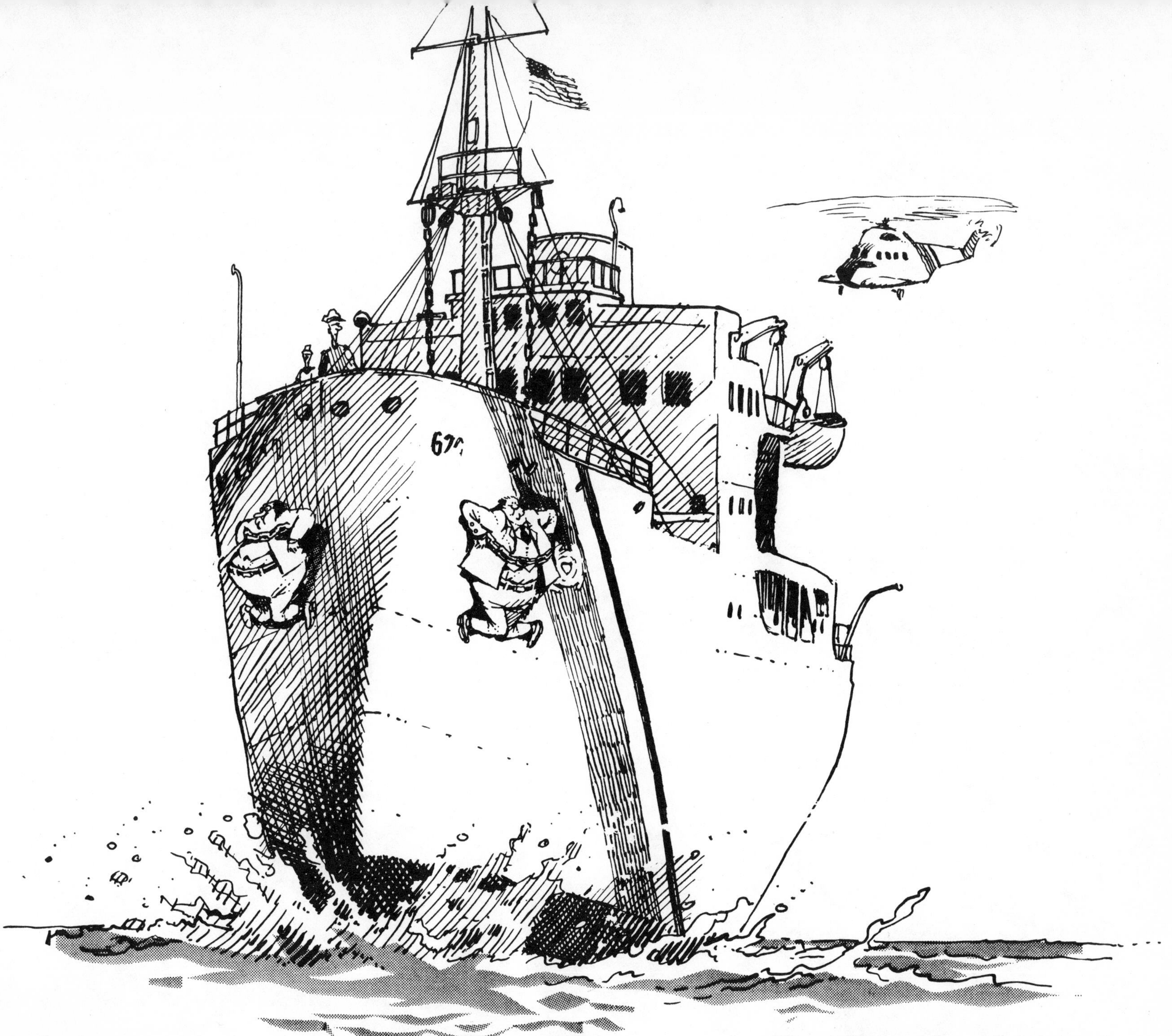

Drug Smugglers' Lawyers

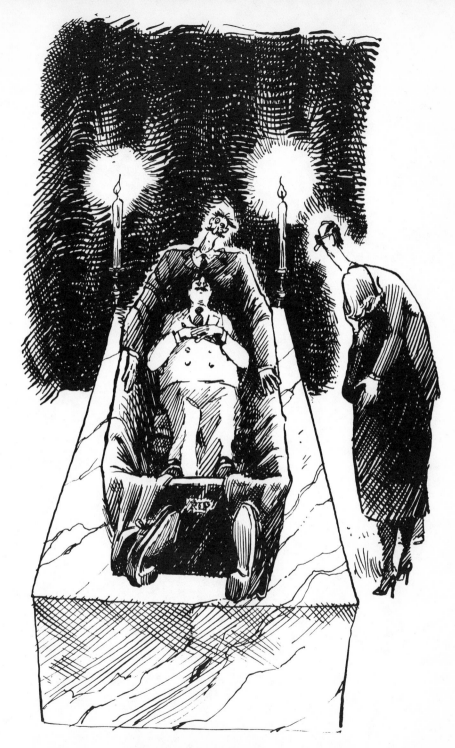

Probate Lawyer

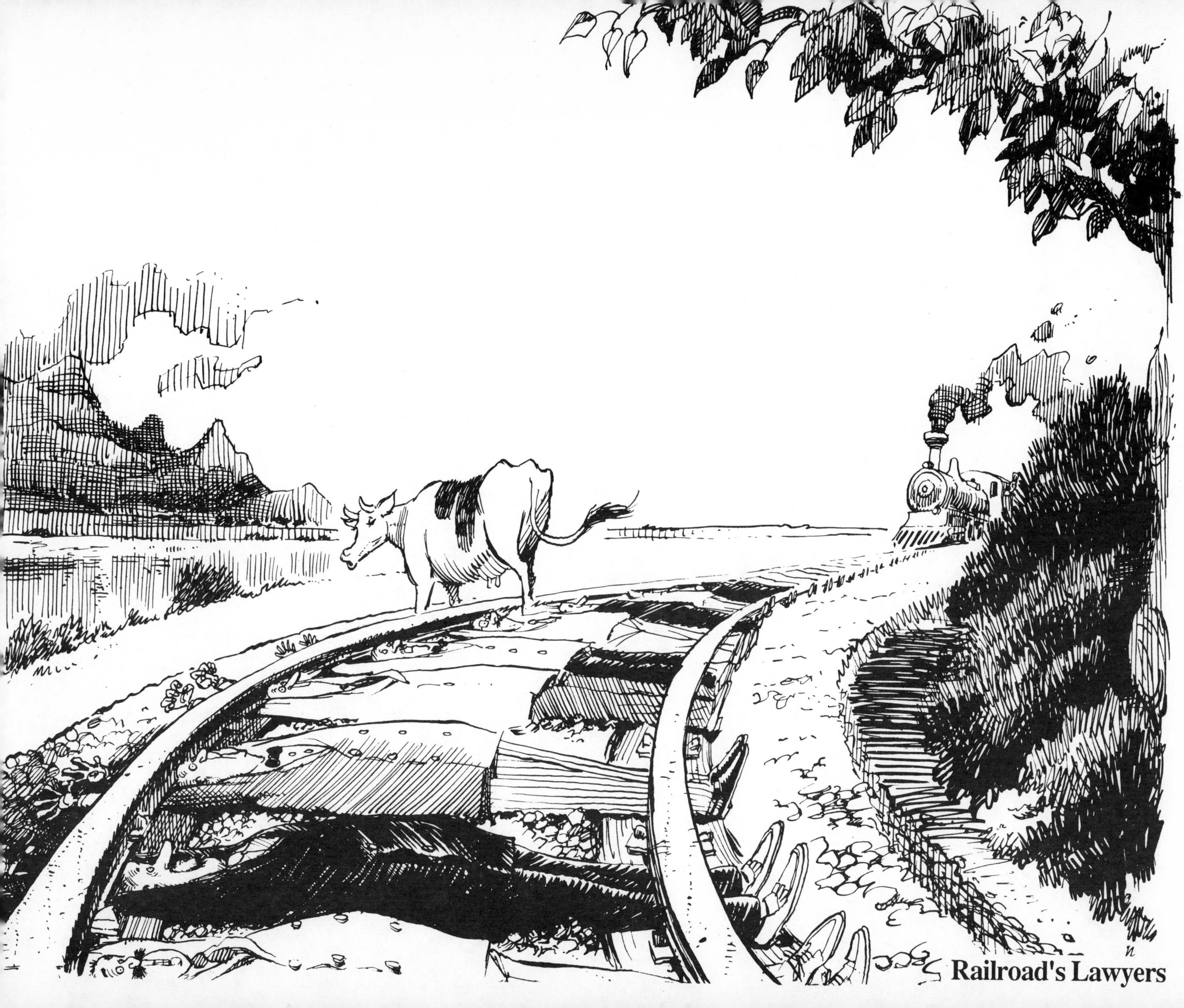

Railroad's Lawyers

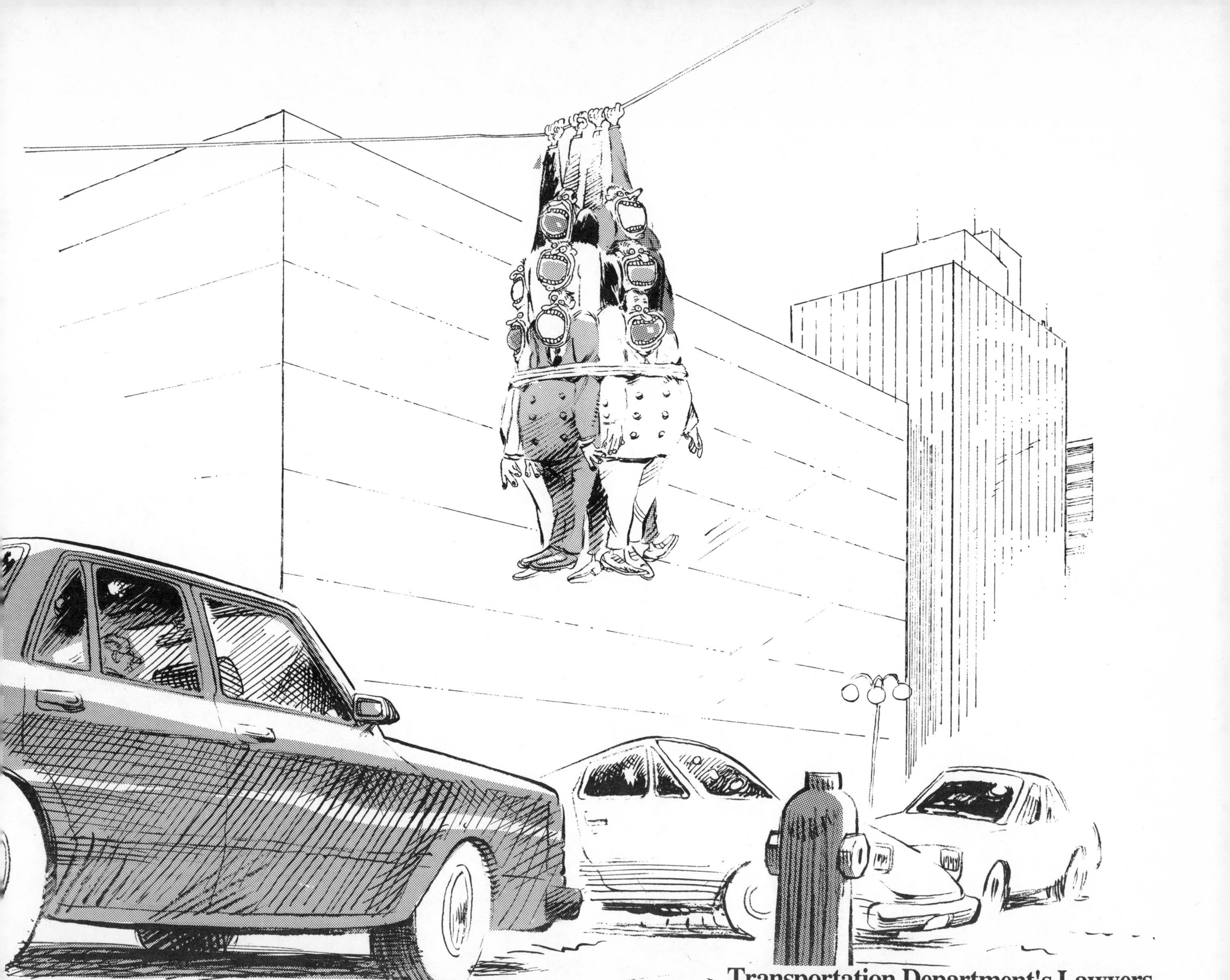

Transportation Department's Lawyers

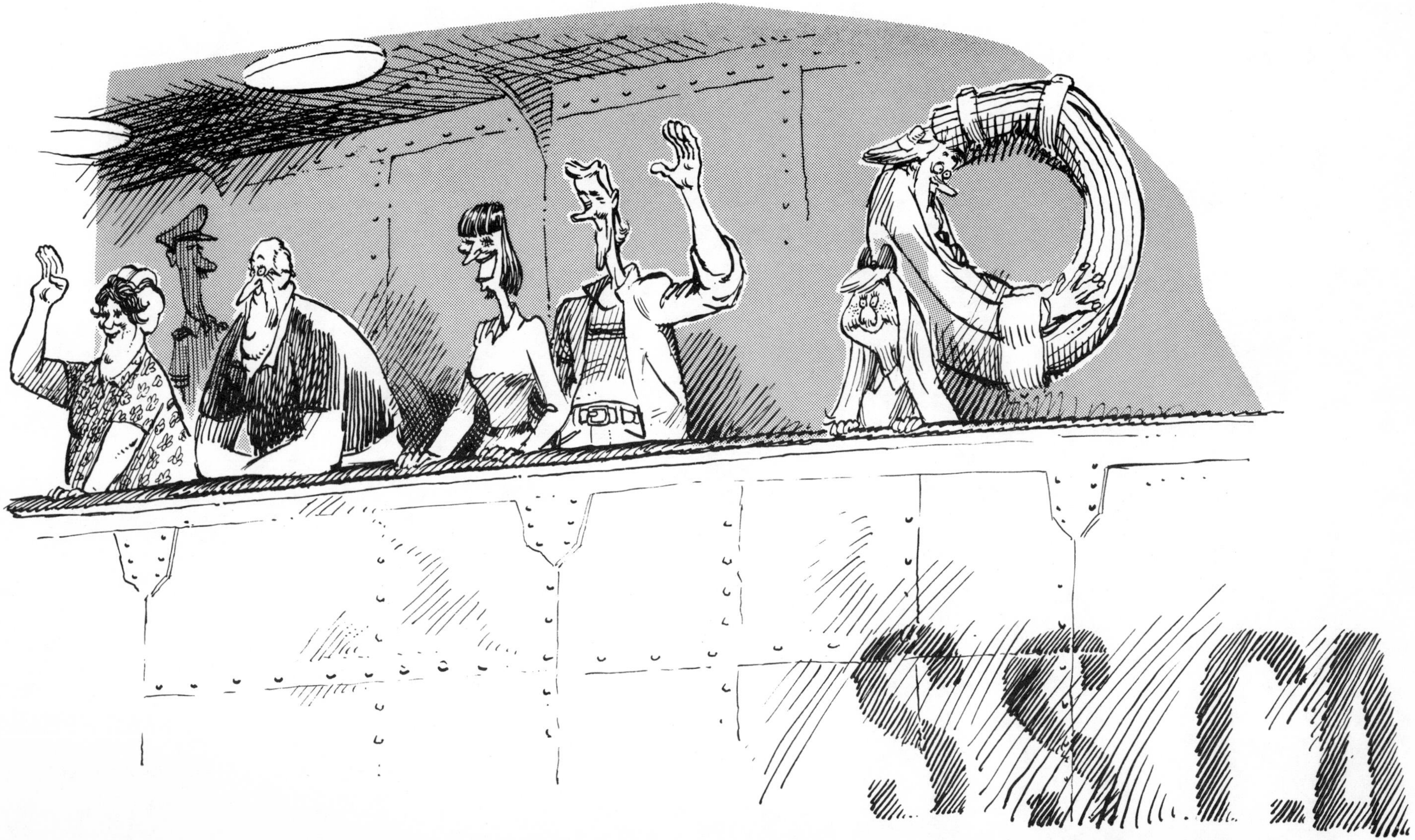

Travel Agent's Lawyer

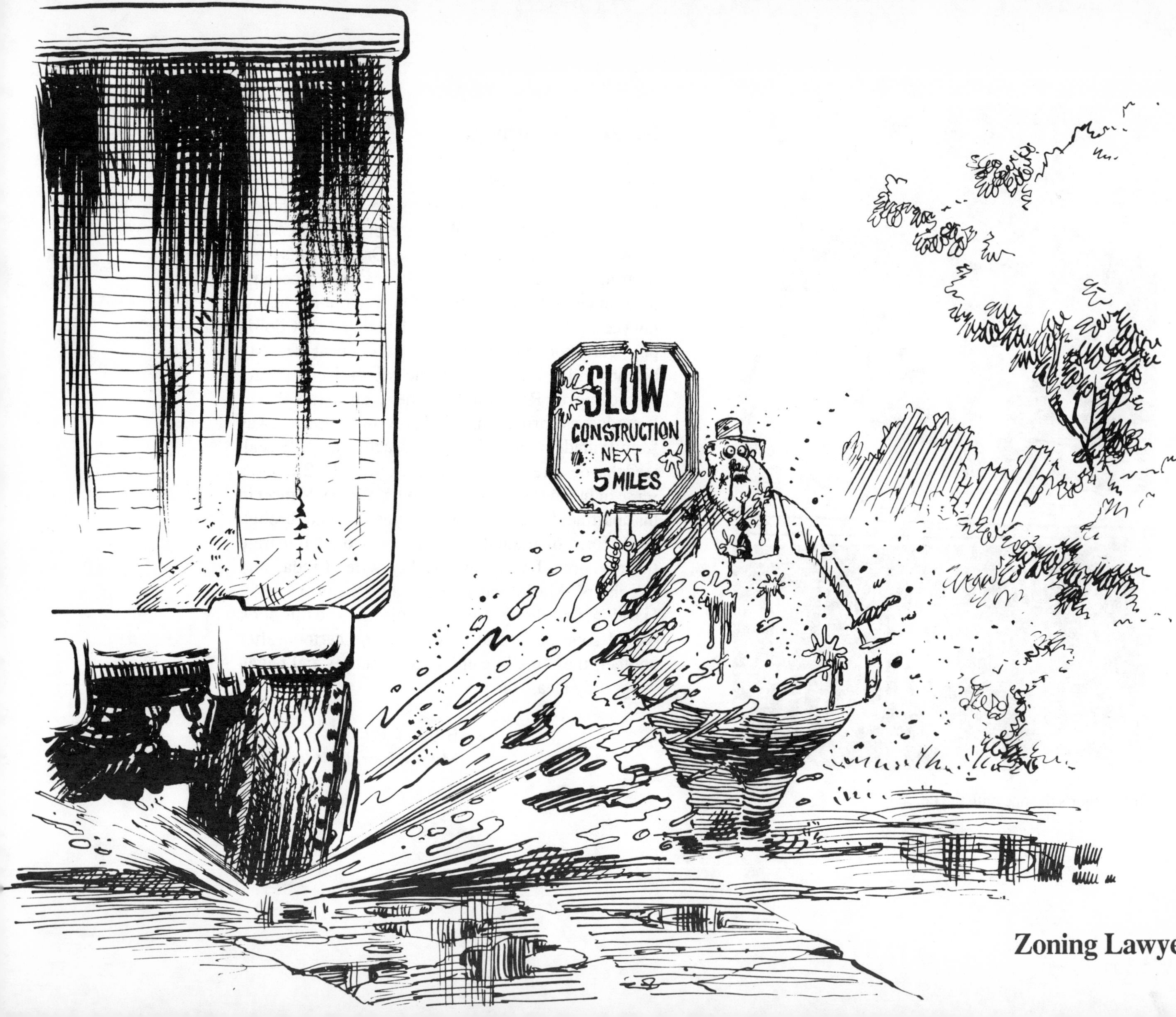
SLOW
CONSTRUCTION
NEXT
5 MILES

Zoning Lawyer

4/04 $2.–

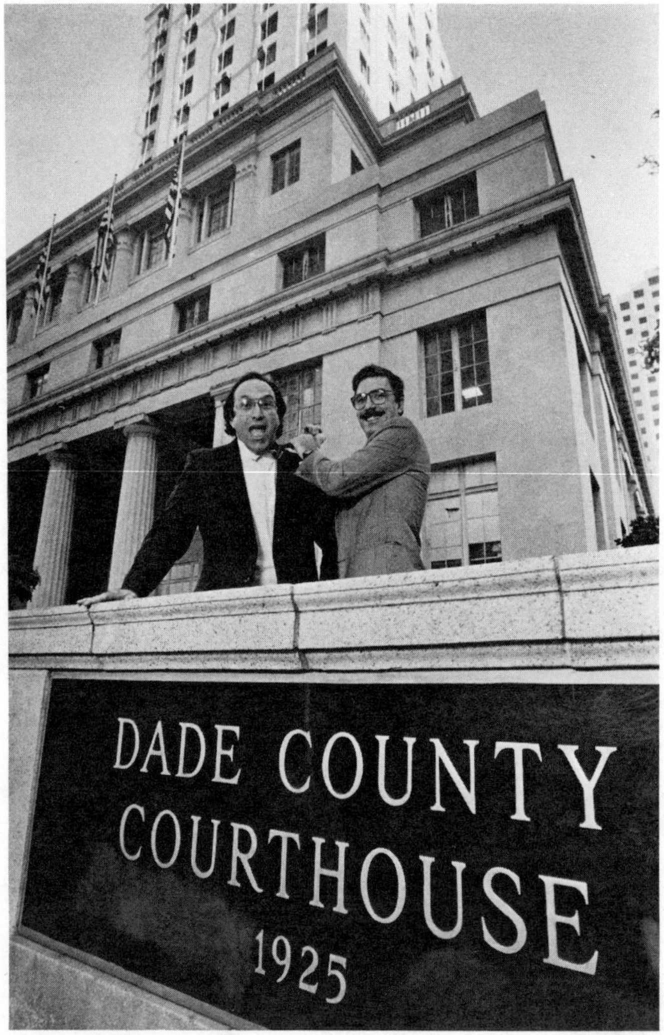
DADE COUNTY
COURTHOUSE
1925

Bill Berger's the one with the tie.

Note on the Authors

Thirteen years as a trial attorney can have a profound effect on one's brain. Perhaps it's the constant competitiveness, the adversarial nature of the profession, the demands of clients and judges. Or maybe it's from wearing neckties all that time. In any case, I became determined to find something funny about my fellow lawyers. After much thought, I realized that doing physically horrible things to them was a neat idea. My brother, Ellis, a reporter at The Miami News, introduced me to Ricardo Martinez, an artist there. Ricardo was born in Chile and grew up in Spain. I was from Philadelphia and Miami Beach. I quickly realized that despite our different backgrounds, Ricardo's sense of humour was as sick as mine. We would meet in his apartment overlooking Biscayne Bay and through some form of mental osmosis, he would illustrate these visions I was having. My wife, Linda, and daughters, Marla and Lauren, and Ricardo's wife, Hazel, at first thought our compulsion to do this book would soon pass. But as we did one cartoon after another, they finally came to their senses and began suggesting ideas, too.

Bill Berger
Miami, Florida